Lady Dawn Annandale

# The Lockdown Diaries

*The Lockdown Diaries*

Published by The Conrad Press in the United Kingdom 2021

Tel: +44(0)1227 472 874
www.theconradpress.com
info@theconradpress.com

ISBN 978-1-913567-99-6

Typesetting and cover design by Charlotte Mouncey, www.bookstyle.co.uk
The Conrad Press logo was designed by Maria Priestley.

Printed and bound in Great Britain by Clays Ltd, Elcograf S.p.A.

We all experience a darkest hour in one form
or another so this silliness is dedicated to my
wonderful friends who helped me see the light.
And, also did all the rank stuff during my bald/
nearly dead/chemotherapy period. Surprisingly,
they are all still my friends despite the puking in
their cars and spare rooms let alone what
I did in their loos. I love you all.

Vanessa M, Emma, Louise, Karyn, Denise,
Chistine, Rachel S, Rachael D, Laura P, Rachel
L-H, Tracy C, Tracey W, Vanessa H, Penny D,
Michaela W, Lucia, Liz, Jackie M, Clairey G.

# Author's note:

Last Christmas, my beloved surpassed himself. Well accustomed to my delusions of grandeur, he asked Santa to bring me a title and an elephant. Actually, as a descendant of King Robert the Bruce I should really have gone the whole hog and opted for Queen. Anyhoo, I am now, wait for it, officially Lady Dawn Annandale through the marvellous work of Scottish Heritage and the lovely people at Dunans Castle. In exchange for a few quid which aids the restoration of this beautiful building, and, as befits my station in life, I am now the proud owner of a square foot of Scotland and I'm a Lady! Oh...the elephant didn't actually come and live with us here in Portugal because that would just be silly. We called him Noel and decided he was better off in Africa with his mum so we just send some pennies to the World Wildlife Fund to feed him. Funnily enough, Noel quite likes fermented fruit which isn't that surprising really.

**THANK YOU**

Lady Dawn Annandale

You're helping WWF to protect the future of wild elephants and to tackle some of the biggest environmental challenges facing our natural world today.
Thank you.

Paul De Ornellas
Chief Adviser – Wildlife, WWF-UK

Hello, I'm Dawn. I live in the Algarve with my beloved, Rodney, between four and six cats and varying numbers of transient children with or without their partners who we will hereinafter refer to as 'Brat no…' insert as appropriate. There are six of the little monsters, all with their various entourages. I'm not the maternal type so please don't ask me their ages or even names because at my advanced age it's an uphill struggle to remember my own name let alone all that horrid lot. And, it was a long time ago I chose their names so how am I supposed to recall something from twenty-five years ago when I was most probably drunk?

2020 will forever be one of those memorable years. I can see us now; wrapped up in a crocheted blanket in a nursing home with my friend Rachel, repeating ourselves for the thirty-seventh time to our great-grandchildren. We were there - ooooh, and we even ran out of loo roll or equally exciting anecdotes which encourages the kids to reach for a pillow and up the morphine. 2021 continues to be another very peculiar year with Brexit, Covid, Trump, Bojo, aliens and general Book of Revelations stuff. Personally, we try not to let any of that stuff interfere with the more pressing, daily struggles such as 'what shall we have for supper?' and 'we've run out of cat food.'

I started writing this in March (I think) when the whole death, doom and destruction thing started. Actually, it was probably after running out of loo roll, wondering why, then turning the telly on to watch the news and seeing a rather rotund orange chap talking about 'Chinese flu'.

Our little bubble of sunshine and pussy-cats hasn't really changed that much because we are generally lazy, anti-social, old (although we like to pretend we're terribly hip and groovy), we are in fact probably a tiny bit vulnerable. Rod doesn't want to have a vaccine because he thinks Bill Gates will turn him off when he's seventy via some kind of chip injected with the vaccine. That would be rather a shame as he hasn't finished the extension yet. Personally, I don't think Bill knows who Rod is so I'm still looking at new curtains and bathroom tiles. I had a fairly yukky bout of breast cancer and all that gungy stuff that goes with it – I looked like Uncle Fester at one stage then progressed to a loo brush finally moving on to a Kevin Keegan perm circa 1975. So, we use that as an excuse to stay in bed and watch all manner of rubbish day-time telly and call it 'resting' when it's more lazyitus.

The following diary entries are a combination of philosophical musings and utter tripe which I hope will a) educate you as to the inner workings of a middle-aged, menopausal woman and b) give you something to laugh at.

## Day 1

Feels weird to have to stay home and not be able to do the usual stuff. It's been an odd day - there was no *Homes Under the Hammer* for a start which threw us completely so we were up before 11am for a change. Anyway, I finished painting these amazing chandeliers (gold obvs) we bought at the auction. Rod put them up in our new bedroom in the extension which is coming along nicely. You will note that my delusions of grandeur have not subsided as obviously everyone should have two chandeliers in their bedroom darhling.

Planted stuff. Can't remember what is where because I'm not an organised kind of person and like surprises. Weeded the garden with the help of a Dick Francis audiobook (don't judge me) and a vodka and tonic. We did have a quick discussion about whether the sun was over the yardarm but decided it most definitely was and it's also totally flexible so doesn't actually matter.

First big problem of the day came to light when I had a bath after all that gardening - it was hot so I was smelly and think I knelt in cat poo at some stage. Once I'd dug out all the muck from beneath my pink sparkly nails, I was horrified to see I've broken a nail. Super glue to the rescue and my heart stopped pounding.

Did a roll call with the kids - well, I just said 'alive?' in our family WhatsApp group which shows what a compassionate mother I am.

Took my cannabis oil, at about 7pm, then Spag Bol for dinner accompanied by a very small glass of red vino (I think the cats must drink the wine when we go to bed - those 5litre wine boxes only last a couple of days).

Bed to watch *Ozark* on Netflix. Cannabis Oil started to do its magical thing and I drifted off into a world of mellow funny feelings so it was time to sleep. All in all, a pretty normal day here in the Algarve.

Lady Dawn Annandale

*Day 2*

Started with the usual 'whose turn is it to make the tea?' thing and luckily Rod's need was greater than mine because he needed a pee first and put the kettle on. Caught up with the news and felt a bit sad about no *Homes Under the Hammer* again but decided that being productive and alighting from the boudoir before 11am is probably a good thing.

You know that morning after gardening thing? Felt like my bottom and thighs had aches inside and don't get me started on my back!

Roll call with the brats went well - only Charlie decided to be silly, stupid boy. Do you have the same conversations every day? We do. We did the breakfast one, then the 'what are we doing today?' one followed by 'what would you like for dinner?' - it's less exciting than it sounds.

Rod did the caveman thing and went off in search of provisions and cement or plaster or something whilst I (being vulnerable and delicate) stayed at home away from human beans. If this had been two thousand years ago I guess he would have gone off with a spear and a chariot but he just took credit cards and made sure there was plenty of diesel.

Surveying my domain, i.e., the kitchen, I decided to empty all the cupboards and the bar and clean and tidy them. And, take everything from the shelves, wash, dust, rearrange and actually do it properly. So I did. Found eight slow cookers, three boxes of chocolate fingers, two lost cake tins, a thousand piece jigsaw and the reason a drawer wouldn't shut - Spider-Man cake toppers were jammed in the back. There were t-lights and batteries, an empty biscuit tin and the Christmas serviettes, pens, and the best find, a miniature bottle of gin!

The bar was a bit of a different story - very sad in fact. There were about twenty empty bottles so the recycling will be happy! Think it's a combination of our short-sightedness and general inebriation that had led to about six bottles of the same thing being opened at once - yes I know; who has six bottles of gin opened at the same time... Anyway, it's all tidy and there are now gaps in the bar which need refilling at the earliest possible opportunity.

Whilst I was being the perfect 1950's housewife, Rod was on a mission to do his good deed for the day. He found a wallet with over €2,000 inside and basically the chap's life - has anyone ever tried to obtain a replacement drivers license in Portugal?? So he did some detective work and returned the wallet to the chap. Gold star darling.

Off Rod went to play with his new toys - plaster and cement and that expanding foam stuff - must be like having a play dough session for chaps.

What with beef stew in the slow cooker, fresh flowers in the bedroom and dusting, I really do think the whole sun/yardarm question is now irrelevant especially as I had to dust the bar too and vodka definitely aids housework.

Disaster struck after dinner when the telly was switched on - no internet!! Sensing a long and fraught night, I took a few extra drops of my magic potion in an effort to cope with the calamity and potential grumpiness of his not being able to watch the telly. Now, bearing in mind that between us we have the technical capability of an ant, I was quite resigned to listening to an audiobook with my knitting. But, after about two hours of guessing and poking and that old favourite, turn it off and on again, we managed an episode of *Ozark*.

Seriously, two days in and I'm already blaming cabin fever for the increase in Smirnoff's share values and my cannabis oil consumption. Two days...

Dawn aged 3

# Day 3

Thought I'd be really helpful today and tidy up the shed. Well, I say shed but in reality it's a little house in the garden where the washing machine lives with all the detritus of our lives. I took everything out - our bikes, (mine's an electric one which goes some way to explaining the size of my bottom). Rod puts things in the shed on the nearest available space, as men do, but was still pleasantly surprised when I found three tape measures, about six trowels, floats, paintbrushes, enough screws and nails to supply B&Q for a year and I lost count of how many tubes of silicon. We did have a very exciting trip to the municipal skip in the car - been the highlight of the week! Dumped the rubbish off, filled up the recycling without shame for a change because no-one else was there to witness my alcoholic tendencies, and went home without seeing another car or person.

The cats are taking the piss now. There's always one trying to come in the house or squeaking for food, as bad as kids but a bit cheaper I suppose. Nigella peed on a rug the other day - it's a while since any of the kids have done that to be fair. Definitely think Terry is pregnant - oh joy! Even more bloody cats!

Did the roll call thing - kids all eventually checked in. I think they think it's funny to keep me guessing but they forget I have spares so it's not quite the same as having an only child - always one in reserve. They all seem to be working from home or whatever other euphemism for watching Netflix they concoct.

G&T was delivered to me in the bath whilst I was listening to an Agatha Christie audiobook and scraping the muck from under my nails. A peaceful half-an-hour of de-hairing, exfoliating and trying to decide on what to make for dinner.

After a family size portion of spag bol - another reason my bottom is so vast - I left Rod eating his Victoria sponge and was in bed by 8.15 with my knitting.

It's all a bit surreal - not being able to go to a bar or restaurant, visit friends etc. But, on the plus side we are all going to have the cleanest, tidiest house, all those little jobs he's been promising to do for the last three years will finally be done and maybe even have time for reading, hobbies etc. We may even actually talk to each other at some stage!

Terry, Nigella and Duncan. The Ginger Pussy only turns up at night - I don't even like cats...

*Day 4*

Mothering Sunday so obviously I had to speak to the brats. They sent me links to BoJo's speech about staying away from the elderly to keep them safe - so thoughtful.

We seem to have broken the internet thingy because it won't work in the kitchen any more. Tried googling 'why won't the repeater work so I can watch *Bargain Hunt*?' but gave up because whoever writes those technical answers clearly does not take into account people who remember black and white telly.

Decided to make something a bit different for dinner so bunged loads of stuff in the slow cooker and made a red Thai curry sauce. Spent a delightful hour or so peeling prawns then my absolute favourite job of slicing them open and cleaning out the poo.

Had a trip to Lidl for vital supplies, (vodka) and was amazed at how sensible and respectful the people here in the Algarve are towards one another especially those who are working in the supermarkets. People are keeping their distance, staying a safe distance apart, Lidl had everything as normal and no one was buying more than necessary.

Rod made very unsubtle hints about having eaten the last slice of cake the previous night so I knocked up a quick Victoria sponge whilst sampling a very tiny vodka and tonic and listening to yet another Dick Francis audiobook.

Dinner was amazingly wonderful even if I do say so myself.

Served the prawn curry with couscous - not a speck of leftovers. Managed to spill red wine over a clean white table cloth which I have just remembered I forgot to soak last night, which is nice.

Nellie, Ju, Charlie Bunny, Sach, Tilly La-La, Jim-Jam, love you all the green cheese on the moon.

Small Brats

*Day 5*

Monday is currently my favourite day of the week purely for the new series of Outlander. Felt quite self-indulgent (for all of thirty seconds) as I stayed in bed until about midday watching Jamie and Claire Frazer fight the baddies.

Reality returned and had to drag myself out of bed to do housewifely stuff. We don't usually have breakfast until about midday so after porridge and honey (Rod) and a fish-finger sandwich with poached eggs and horse-radish (me) I did the dishwasher, chucked a chicken in the oven, put the washing out and cleaned the bathrooms.

Having spilled yet another glass of wine over yet another white tablecloth boring stuff like bleaching and washing had to be done. Having been doing this washing/cleaning/cooking stuff for about thirty-five years now, I'm on autopilot and just go through the motions. However, think it must be the menopause or possibly just old age but lately I seem to be losing things, (where did I put that bottle of vodka?) or putting things away in the wrong place (vodka doesn't live in the microwave) or running out of things when I think there is plenty (who drank all the vodka?) so I've decided to go through the cupboards before we go shopping and, write a list and, remember to take said list.

Listened to the rest of my Agatha Christie audiobook whilst stripping the chicken for a salad, (tonight) chicken, mushroom and leek pie (tomorrow night) and the bits went in the slow cooker for soup. I try very hard to feed us properly (with the exception of my fish-finger obsession) and to eat loads of vegetables and making everything from scratch (apart from filo pastry - life's too short). Judging from the extent of the methane emissions from our bottoms I think I generally succeed.

Rod went off in search of architrave for our lovely new bedroom whilst I blackened the newly installed wood burner. By the time he returned the sun/yardarm was in full swing and a tiny, understated V&T was helping me prepare the salad.

I had a wander around the garden, deadheading the roses and marigolds, petunias and fuchsias. In the stillness of the lockdown, I could hear bumble bees and birds, no traffic noises, chickens and sheep in the distance. It's rather lovely to notice so much wildlife instead of missing it because we are going out or too busy. We have this overgrown area of garden, which is next on the to-do list, full of wild flowers like these beautiful purple poppies and thistles. Picked some poppy heads and threw them amongst the flower beds hoping they might flower next year.

Much to my delight I found an unopened and forgotten 5litre wine box in a kitchen cupboard which, like all Portuguese wine, was delicious. And, it was about €8 which is quite marvellous.

Had dinner and listened to BoJo explaining the UK lockdown which will hopefully help contain this dreadful situation or at least stagger the casualties so that the NHS isn't totally overwhelmed.

Took a few extra drops of magic potion tonight as feeling a bit achy and sore - any excuse! Off to bed with snoring beauty; my headphones and Agatha Christie. Stay home everyone and look after each other.

*Day 6*

Managed to poke myself up my nose whilst drinking our morning cup of tea delivered by the maid (Rod) and, after not even spilling the tea, noticed my nails are like bloody talons. Pale pink sparkly talons which really need in-fills aren't particularly attractive, so if there are any nail ladies out there with a hazmat suit could you pop over please? It's not just nails but hair needs a cut, not to mention a colour, bit of waxing wouldn't go amiss because there's nothing worse than a bird with a tash.

It feels like Ground-hog Day doesn't it? Apart from having something different for dinner each night. Talking of which, I've been really housewifely this week and googling recipes. So, chicken, leek and mushroom pie with shortcrust pastry with mashed potatoes. Chucked carrots in with the potatoes and fried onions and cheese. Rather scrummy.

The extension is coming along marvellously. You know things are progressing when you install a bar in your bedroom. It's all gold and sparkly and matches those tiny chandeliers so perfectly. The sofas are gold too - looks a bit like King Midas' holiday home but we like it!

Surpassed myself with a spectacular tripping over whilst carrying a two litre decanter of red wine. Yep, face down in that lot; blood, wine, glass and me. Rod picked me up, no cranes involved, and after picking out a few bits of glass I'm lucky to have escaped with my thumb being slashed open badly but I'll live. Arm and thigh banged but all that padding comes in useful sometimes!

The brats all checked in - they are working from home where they can, allegedly. I'm so pleased they are all being good and staying home which is harsh financially especially for the brat with hair/beauty salons.

Went to bed with a stiff drink, purely for medicinal purposes, watched *Ozark* then the news. All those people crammed into the tubes! Is it really worth the risk?? I think mortgages should be suspended, rent suspended, utility bills suspended, council tax and business rates. The only really important thing is that everyone has enough to eat surely? Oh, and Netflix so you don't die of boredom!

Due to popular demand I picked loads of poppies and will post the seeds off to those who asked. It did occur to me that this could be the start of a heroin distribution network but hopefully if I am arrested the nice judge will understand that Cindy and Maggie are not drug lords but housewives who like gardening and the colour purple.

Drifted off in my magic potion induced sleep with an extra few drops to help me sleep after my bump.

## Day 1

Woke up feeling very battered and bruised after my little disagreement with the decanter and the floor last night but the tea fairy (Rodders) was kind and arrived to ease the pain. I have the most amazing bruise on my thigh which is a lovely shade of purple which I'm sure you would all like to see. I'll attempt to take a picture of it, avoiding bottom and knickers I promise.

Eventually dragged myself out of bed and made some breakfast then had a bath. Did the whole thing one handed and despite poking myself in the eye with mascara and having black stuff all over the place, I vaguely managed.

Making a lasagne was a bit of a challenge. Especially the bit where I broke a nail and couldn't find the pink sparkly half that pinged off as I stirred the cheese sauce but, no one mentioned any crunchy bits so it must have been OK.

A lovely friend left us a box of tangerines fresh from his tree which are fabulous - wonderful to have such thoughtful people around us.

We had our daily ongoing argument with the internet. Well, I say we but I really mean Rod because I have not a Scooby what any of the googled sites are actually talking about. I only ever talk to Alexa and ask her nicely to play *The Archers* or, in preparation for our last gang night out at Chicken Luis then the karaoke, Alexa helpfully put 'Ob-La-DI, Ob-La-Da' on repeat for me to learn the words. It's all too hard so I just made a chocolate and ginger pudding instead.

Extension going really well. We now have a rather smart bedroom door, skirting boards and moving on to the hallway and ceilings. Fab to see it all coming together. Decided on a colour for the kitchen - parrots. We love a parrot - Captain Flint and Molly live in the main kitchen with parrot stuff popping up all over the place. Saw this parrot fabric and thought I could cover the kitchen units in it with a blue wall and a red wall to match. What do you think?

Didn't drop or spill or break anything for a change which makes pleasant change. Toodled off to bed, gave up on *Ozark* because snoring beauty fell asleep. Plugged my headphones in and listened to an ancient *Sherlock Holmes* radio play and dreamt of Long John Silver being on *Masterchef*. I blame the magic potion...

# Day 8

Don't know about a cup of tea this morning - could have done with a triple Bloody Mary! Felt like I'd had an argument with a steam roller and lost. Having fallen flat on my face and jarring knees, elbows, ribs, thigh etc. feel a very poorly sausage. Was so stiff, sore, and achy that actually leaving bed was just not something I wanted to do. But, being the brave soldier I am (and needing a wee) at about half twelve I emerged to make some breakfast.

Spoke to the brats - I think they only phoned to check on any advances on their inheritance. I reassured them I wasn't about to expire any time soon and they all managed to stifle their disappointment.

I already make those noises that old people do when they stand up or sit down or move generally. Always accompanied of course by, ooooh, my back... in that pathetic little sad voice. So, after discovering my red wine and blood soaked dress, t shirt and towel in the washing basket and dumping them in bleach, put the other washing out and went back to bed.

Few catch-up phone calls later it seemed acceptable to pour a medicinal V&T and take a beer up to Rod working hard putting flooring down in the extension. I supervised for about half an hour before deciding it was time to have another little rest.

Raked through the freezer and found nice things to nuke. Fed the cats, fed us and went to bed amidst faffing about like trying to mould about eight pillows around me to make it all comfy. Lots and lots of magic potion tonight - any excuse at all obvs and about three minutes of telly before my beloved was in the land of nod. Turned the telly off and went to sleep with Sherlock Holmes foiling yet another dastardly escapade. By popular demand, my poorly thigh.

When your cat watches too much Master Chef...

## Day 9

Little bit of cabin fever is setting in. We went to the DIY shop and I just sat in the car for the sake of going out. Driving to a builders merchant and home again is obviously not usually my first choice for a day out/exciting adventure but don't knock it until you're in lockdown. It's a ghost town out there - a few cars but no people. Hardly anyone at the builders merchant - just a few chaps keeping as far away from one another as possible and focused on the joy of finally having something to do when they arrive home with their bags of cement and other blokey stuff.

Fed the cats yet again. Terry is definitely pregnant - actually saw a bump moving on the side of her expanding tummy. Duncan seems to be hanging around with Terry most of the time so I hope these new parents know what they are letting themselves in for - all that joy and happiness, poverty and parents evenings.

Watered the garden and am delighted and possibly a bit too excited at the emergence of tiny carrots and onions, courgettes, lettuce and aubergines. Millions of tomatoes on the vines which is lovely to see. Herbs coming along nicely too - mint, chives, coriander and basil. Think I must have been a witch in a previous life as I really like growing stuff and making potions.

Dinner was spectacular (even if it was a bit spicy and woke Rod up in the night and made him run to the loo). Sliced steak thinly, chucked it in a wok with onions, garlic, chilli powder, courgettes, kidney beans, red peppers and fried it all together. Served with warm fajitas, lots of cheese, rice and a dressing made from mascarpone, chilli, lemon juice, red peppers and garlic. One positive from all this is having time to mess about with new recipes and make something a bit different for supper.

Opened the last bottle of red. Highlight of tomorrow is obviously going to be replenishing stocks. It has been pointed out to me that a 5 litre wine box is supposed to last the week and is not to be construed as a challenge.

Magic potion, bed, *Ozark*, tried to sleep, couldn't, Rod restless so more *Ozark* until 3am. Sleep until 12.00! How lazy! It feels interminable so more effort needs to be put into actually maintaining normality - having breakfast at 1pm is a tad late even for us!

A very pregnant Terrence.

## Day 10

Whilst Rod went off to the DIY shop again, I didn't. Staying in bed seemed a much more pleasant alternative, so I did. When the wanderer returned it was breakfast time (more like afternoon tea in reality) so porridge for Rodders and I had chicken pie because I'm such a rebel.

By the time we had finished and the dishwasher was on, it was about half two and I had to think about dinner. Chucked loads of stuff in the slow cooker and hoped for the best.

Spoke to the brats (see, I can do this mother stuff) - Brat no.3 has regressed and had spent the day playing x box with his chums whilst Brat no.6 has worked out that having two beautiful huskies gets him out of the house for lots of walks.

The garden and driveway does look a bit like Steptoe's yard so decided to have a proper tidy up - the kind where you end up at the tip and break a nail. Shooed all the bloody cats away and stacked the logs in the kitchen, found a packet of seeds, planted them, swept up, then moved the six ft water cylinder that was blocking the kitchen door to a more practical space before it's installed upstairs. A car full of rubbish and recycling later, the garden considerably less Steptoe and on its way to Kew.

By 5pm I still wasn't dressed so thought it was a bit late to bother. Sun over yardarm obvs so a large G&T and a beer for my beloved seemed a jolly good idea. We sat and watched the view over Loule and Faro - you could hear a pin drop. The silence brings it all home to you - when you remember why it's so silent you want to weep.

Temperature dropped at about 7.30pm so Rod lit the wood burner and the heat and cosiness of the kitchen cheered me up a bit. After dinner I just wanted to go to bed with a bit of escapism and forget all the horrible stuff going on in the world. Had my magic potion and watched *Ozark* which is such a brilliant series. Snoring beauty just about managed to reach the end of the episode so I turned the telly off and googled chicken recipes on YouTube.

Feeling a bit sad and worried but eternally hopeful for the human race.

Missing the brats today. Not much, just a little bit.

Brat no. 3 and 4, Rod and me

# Day 11

Totally lost track of the days of the week. There's no structure and frankly it's so unimportant now anyway. Only the cats seem to be relentless with breakfast, lunch and dinner to keep us on track. It was a 'couldn't be arsed' kind of day so I shamefully admit that breakfast was at about 1.00 pm.

In a desperate attempt at creating variety, Rod had homemade lemon and ginger marmalade instead of porridge whilst we decided what exciting activities we should pass the day doing.

We needed a trip to the supermarket and have been told that you are only allowed to go to your nearest one so off we went to Lidl in Loule. Amazingly, I looked through the cupboards and fridge before we went and I even checked that there were plenty of bags for life in the car! All this time on my hands is turning me into an organised middle aged woman complete with trolley token. Very uncomfortable - I always envisaged being slightly more rock and roll and less Radio 4 but one has to adapt I suppose.

Lidl was fully stocked and virtually empty of people with the few there being terribly polite and maintaining the two metre thingy. Never thought I would class a trip to Lidl as a day out but that's how it felt as I savoured the luxury of having loads of time to properly examine those stretchy bras my friends swear by.

Brats are fine. I noted their comments - see below - and will think of another way to embarrass them ASAP.

Had some shopping to buy for a friend so after dropping our own shopping off at home, popped over to our friends house to deliver to her back doorstep. Feels odd not observing the usual social niceties of a hug or a kiss or shaking hands but just standing there like a lemon saying hello. Funny the daft things we miss. Still, we did our good deed for the day and then poodled off home.

I've been planting loads of vegetables over the last couple of weeks and am so excited about the little shoots popping up. Carrots, aubergines, courgettes, lettuce, tomatoes, onions, peppers, chillies are all coming along nicely so bought radish, spinach, parsley and basil. I'm a rubbish gardener and learning all the time but it is made easier by the copious amounts of sunshine here.

Samuel Whiskers is unhappy for some reason. We have a rat who lives behind the bar in the kitchen with his wife and kids. I leave them dinner of carrots and apples behind a gap in the skirting board. Cheeky little bugger pushed a piece of apple back out and the next day wouldn't eat his carrot! Cats are useless - don't seem to have noticed the bloody rats. Bunch of freeloaders and with the imminent arrival of Terrence's babies, we'll have even more mouths to feed.

I made fried chicken for dinner with chips and salad. It was almost like KFC only KFC doesn't serve red wine and, such a surprise, I do.

Loving going to bed early to watch telly and being lazy. Must admit it seems earlier each day and my cannabis oil dose seems to be increasing every day. Purely for medicinal reasons of course.

## Day 12

Started planting things then it rained tigers and wolves here in the Algarve. Radish and lots of herbs for my new herb garden (haven't actually mentioned this bit to Rod yet) which will hopefully comprise of basil, parsley, coriander, and other stuff which I can't remember because I threw the packets away. Anyway, I'd started making a mess with the soil and all the pots so thought might as well continue in the rain. Saved my watering it all so every cloud.

Monday is a new episode of Outlander day so that was obvs my biggest priority. Dreadful acting but the scenery is good! I do love an historical drama - all that swashbuckling and rampant sex is really quite marvellous.

Have run out of cupboards to turn out, drawers to tidy and we don't even have a 'man drawer' any more because I threw away those dead batteries, dried up pens and the keys for the last house but six lived in. We now have torches that work on top of the fuse boxes and pens, which actually write, in the office. I threw away the twenty-three thousand odd screws left over from Ikea.

Hot flushes have returned with a vengeance - thought they were finally going to leave me in peace but the little ba\*\*ards creep up on me at night and I feel like someone has thrown a bucket of boiling water over me. It's not nice - quite antisocial really as all I want to do when they strike is take all my clothes off. At least it's only Rod who has to contend with that for the foreseeable; aren't you lucky?!

Couldn't wait to go to bed last night and we watched three episodes of *Ozark*. Think the broccoli and Stilton soup did the job as we seemed to be having a poppy bottom competition throughout the night! One of the bloody cats - Nigella I think but didn't have my glasses on so not sure - was inadvertently shut in the house and rudely woke me up to let it out at about 3am - little sod. And, it's been asleep on the bed so more poxy washing. Not only do they refuse to work, (Samuel Whiskers the rat is still residing behind the bar) but now they are generating laundry which makes me very cross on top of having my (let's face it) very necessary beauty sleep disturbed.

Facebook has become quite silly and vaguely pleasant over the last couple of weeks with lots of daft photos and games being played. Makes a wonderful change from everyone ranting about Brexit so I thought I'd jump on the photo of you as a kid band-wagon and show you this photo of me aged about three. Absolutely rocking that yellow hair ribbon!

*Day 14*

'What shall we have for dinner tonight? ' is a phrase which I say in my head or out loud every day. It's relentless and I have no idea what to make so copped out and raked through the freezer for home-made ready meals. I always make a bit extra of whatever we are having and decided to do the grown up thing recently of actually writing on the lids what's inside rather than playing Tupperware roulette.

With chilli defrosting for Rodders and a veggie spaghetti thing for me I decided to spruce up the kitchen and have a paint. I'm a really scabby cook and splash stuff everywhere so painted over red wine stains, bolognaise sauce blobs and something yellow which I haven't a clue about. Painted the stone window frames, dirty marks around the wood burner and a drip from an old leak. Kitchen has never been so clean and I even dusted. Don't panic - it's just a sign of the times and not a personality transplant.

Had long chats with girlfriends which was lovely. All we discussed was how crap our nails are, what we are cooking, how bad our roots are and what time each day we have our first drink!

Brats all behaving and keeping busy. I wish they were here and safe and I could look after them then I come to my senses and pour another vodka.

Thought I'd have a go at making some bread but we don't

have any yeast. Found a great recipe, really easy, so had a go. They were really good so will post it below.

During the course of the last two weeks I have received so many sick/funny/rude memes and jokes from very bored friends. You lot are twisted - keep them coming because I now know why we are friends.

Dinner then bed but disaster struck (keep it clean) and the Internet wouldn't connect to the telly in the bedroom. Rod went to sleep and I watched a film on my iPad whilst texting and sending more drivel out into cyberspace.

Thought about this new book I'm supposed to be writing so had better get on with it. The first bit of research I did - can't give the subject away yet - was a riot and only confirmed what marvellous (alcoholic and immoral) friends I am blessed to have. The book is called *The Fall and Rise of the Sunshine Cliteratti Society*. I'll let you know when I need a volunteer to read through before I send it off to the publisher. Any resemblance to living persons is purely deliberate but names will be changed to protect the innocent!

## Day 15

Didn't even know what day it was today and Rod thought it was Easter. Time and days seem to have gone out the window (apart from sun/yardarm obvs - I always know that time!) which I think is a reflection of reality. In the real world we need to coordinate our lives but now it's just a rough guide. It feels like Sunday every day when Monday is a bank holiday.

I tried to be productive and started typing my latest novel. The characters in this book are loosely based on real people and true experiences - I can hear the voices in my head cackling with laughter as my friends relate their wicked/funny/illegal stories to me. Because I'm old and menopausal and easily confused, I'm typing the real names of those dreadfully behaved girlies into the manuscript - and must remember to change the names. I promise girls - I will...for a small fee?

What else did I do that was vaguely useful and didn't involve vodka? Oh yes, tidied up an overgrown and scabby corner or the garden and filled the car up with yet more crap to dump at the local 'bins' as we call it. Gold star for me 🏅 I keep trying to do constructive and I know this is a wonderful opportunity to clean out the cutlery drawer and go through Rod's knicker and sock drawers and chuck out all the holey stuff but it's a bit boring isn't it? I mean yes, there are loads of things to be doing like thinning out the carrots and cleaning the new windows in the extension but....

So, I've bored you enough with tales of pussy cats and planting, cooking and cleaning, gardening and gin. You have all been wonderful and thank you for reading my daft daily diary. Stay safe everyone and I shall leave you with a photo of our beautiful view of Loule, Faro and the sea and count myself lucky to be here in Portugal with everything we need. I'll try and take a photo of us too but it's always a challenge because Rod never knows which bit of the camera to look at. Love and kisses.

Rod and the unicorn

## Day Eleventy - Six

Hi kids, thought you might be so bored you wouldn't mind hearing from me. *Homes Under the Hammer* is on again which is marvellous but, it seems to be from 11-12 which, under normal circumstances, is a bit late even for us but time isn't really a thing any more so breakfast is at about one-ish these days.

I have planted so much - I'll be able to start my own green-grocers in about a month! Loads of little shoots everywhere so looking forward to becoming a farmer once this is all over. Well, maybe a farmer who doesn't do mornings. I have vague ideas about trying to do *The Good Life* but my bottom is significantly larger than Felicity Kendall's so it probably wouldn't count.

Luckily the battery has gone in the scales in the bathroom which is a blessing. Is it only me or have your clothes shrunk lately too? Actually, what clothes? It's been a rotation of dressing gowns (and Rod likes to share them too - see below) although I did put clothes on to go to Lidl. Would have been slightly awkward otherwise.

Am missing the brats a bit. Not much obvs. (They read this drivel so I had better say that.) One of them, can't remember which, said they were coming to stay as soon as they were allowed. Looks like we'll be moving soon *sighs* - only joking darlings...

I've made bread, quiche, chocolate fruit cake, marmalade, carrot orange and ginger soup, drunk enough red wine and vodka (not together, although ...) to float the Titanic (and look how that ended) and washed everything in this entire house. I knew things were bad when I realised there is not one untidy draw in the house. Not one. Not dust - not a speck. So not me.

Watched the clock from 4.57pm today and had my first sip of vodka at 5.01pm which is an improvement on the steak I cooked in beer the other day. I mean, it was about 10am and I was messing about chucking stuff in the slow cooker to make a steak pie and there I was, minding my own business and there it was, half a bottle of beer sitting on the bench. The rest is obvs history. 5litre wine boxes are no longer considered a challenge but more of a work in progress.

Watched *Ozark*, no bloody *Outlander* this week, forced Rod to watch *Love Actually* which he said he hated but I saw him teary eyed at the end bit when Hugh Grant is being all soggy. Love that film, especially the end with all those happy arrivals, not that I ever cry when the brats turn up at Faro airport and I have to pick the buggers up.

We've become grand-pussy-parents to Terry and Duncan. Not seen their offspring yet but Terry is a shit mother because she's always leaving the little sods on their own to go out for dinner or a drink. Harlot.

Extension is coming along nicely - we have a loo and a bath upstairs now. Won't be long before we can move upstairs and anyone who comes to stay can live in the bottom half of the house and we won't have to speak to them.

Hot flushes are off the scale - worse than the night I stayed at Louise's when poor Derek came home from his night shift to find this starkers bald fat bird standing in the snow in the garden. Not bald anymore but everything else is the same.

I'll report back in a week or so in case anything happens you might be remotely interested in. Love to you all from sunny Portugal. Stay safe kids.

I think this dressing gown is particularly fetching on Rodney - I would.

Rod, me and a chicken

*Day* 361,154,885

We seem to be having breakfast at about 2.30pm each day which is probably a bit late even for us. It sort of degenerates after that because after I've cleared up the breakfast things, porridge then toast and lemon and ginger marmalade for Rod and poached eggs for me, I really fancy a vodka and tonic. By 'I really fancy' I actually mean I drank two. Large ones.

Bit weird not doing a proper Passover or Easter (we aren't fussy in this house - bring a bottle and you are sooooo welcome) but I did buy Rod some chocolate stuff so he was a happy bunny.

Cleaned my bathroom properly (as opposed to the 'oh f**k it that'll do' clean I usually do) and tidied the drawers up, found some razors which will be useful in the future deforestation of my legs and other unmentionable bits. My bathroom is a shrine to the local Chinese shop so imagine plastic pink roses, cerise and silver sparkly bath mat and even a pink jug to rinse my hair with - the shower thing is temperamental (probably male) so a good old fashioned jug of water over my increasingly grey hair is much easier. I think the pink loo seat is the piece de resistance - all that's missing is one of those knitted loo roll covers but that's easily rectified. Our other bathroom (Rod's) resembles a Parisian brothel (old habits) complete with chandelier and slut red accessories but, I like it.

Actually had visitors this week - well, I say visitors but it was the sheep and the shepherd who looks after them. He's about

738 and walks with a stick. He's very friendly and always stops on his way home in the field next to us, to make sure I'm OK when I'm in the pool, starkers. Bless him.

Last year, in a fit of unbridled romance, Rod bought half a dozen rose bushes for me as a present for our 7th anniversary. Bless him. A glorious red rose has appeared this week - he seems to think that's earned him a gold star; hmmmm diamond ring maybe???

Nigella seems to have made herself at home. After having a wee in the Galaxy, she's now taken to trying to sleep on Rod's pile of PJ's - she especially likes his tartan ones so perhaps she's actually a McCat? Whatever, she's Rod's best friend and seems to be stalking him which is sweet.

I'm missing all my girlies very, very much so have spent literally hours on the phone to them all. We've all got short nails, white hair and are getting really fat. I love you all. I promise the biggest party ever soon as possible.

My sad news this week is that my darling boy, my beautiful Brat no.6 baby bunny who was set to marry his fabulous 6.5, whose wedding was to be the 3rd June, has had to change the date. I was so excited to be the mother of the groom, Louise was going to make sure I was suitably attired, (yes, leopard print) and behave myself (no vodka before the wedding) but, now because of the shitty virus, the wedding is just the two of them with one witness. Brat no.6 has had a very lucky escape because I had my speech prepared and everything but a huge party is in order ASAP.

Over the weekend I have baked, written, gardened, gossiped, cooked, cleaned, nattered, cried, laughed, and loved. Hang on in there kids, it will be OK, eventually.

## Day: Absolutely No F** king Idea

**B**ig day today - so excited to go out. Did a really thorough prep, you know, a DIY pedicure first with one of those foot sander things. Next was a shave of all hairy bits (gross - sorry) because there's nothing worse than a bird with a moustache so it had to go. Legs, feet (yes...) then I was ready.

Trying to do everything in one hit so recycling (I swear that all those bottles weren't just me) and rubbish, garage for petrol (which seems to be evaporating - not being used) and a gas bottle. Then the chemist which was fun. Big queue behind me all two meters apart, me praying that the people behind me don't speak English as I yelled into the intercom to the pharmacist answers to her questions about my ailments and yes please could I have the stuff for menopausal spots and a regular size tub of laxatives would be great and no, I don't need hooking up with a counsellor, could I just have my bloody antidepressants and no I'm not suicidal but the pills help my hot flushes. Fan-bloody-tastic.

Popped a pill as soon as I was back in the car - hot flushes causing me to be sweatiest, smelliest person ever so it would be nice not to stink for a change. Currently wearing more makeup than the Joker to hide my spots so really looking forward to going home, scraping foundation off and smothering my spotty face in anti-menopausal spotty face gunge. Noooicccceee.

Went to Lidl and joined the queue. It's actually wonderful to have a change of scene even if it is just to buy spuds and cat food.

A nice chap called Walter came to see us today about sorting out the interweb thingy so that I can listen to Dick Francis audiobooks all over the house. We tried to explain what we needed and he seemed to understand our total technical inability to explain about WiFi thingys and gigs wotsits. I want to listen to the Archers whilst in the pool - not too much to ask? Can't think why young Walter WiFi man laughed at us.

Brats are fine - one is soooo bored, one is working normally from home, one is enjoying his PlayStation and I can't remember what the others said. I did cry lots and was all snotty and gross after one of them, no.6 I think, told me about his Lockdown wedding. I shall be watching on FaceTime in my big hat, sobbing, bottle of Smirnoff. Gutted I can't be there but hey ho.

Noticed that conversations with brats/girlfriends/Rod seem to focus on what's for dinner tonight because there is nothing else to talk about (apart from conversations with Morag, Emma, Louise, and Karyn which all focus on sex and other dreadful things) so pepper chicken and rice followed by butterfly cakes is in the menu today.

Stay well my friends - we need the biggest party ever after all this!

Leaving you with a dressing gown/pj snog.

## Day: Vodka & Tonic

Shall we play 'I'm more bored than you' Top Trumps. Rod and I played charades, just the two of us and no; that's not a euphemism. Seriously, he did *Casablanca*, *Mama Mia* and *The Man in the Grey Flannel Suit*. Sadly, Rod wouldn't let me film him doing his spectacular depiction of The Battle of the Bulge. Has anyone managed to participate in anything more excruciatingly painful?

Had our Algarve Writing Group meeting over the inter-web. It was great to speak to everyone and see some fresh faces. I did feel a bit ashamed (only a bit, 2/10) that everyone else was actually dressed and I wasn't. Well, I say 'wasn't ' but obviously I wasn't naked because that would be weird. They all did study, clothes, water whilst I was more bed, dressing gown, vodka. All went well and I didn't traumatise anyone by flashing anything inappropriate which is a rare achievement for me.

We both badly need a haircut. In fact, I might attack Rod's mop with the scissors tomorrow and he can put a dye on my inch long, graveyard-blonde, old lady locks. The nice lady at the hairdressers usually does my eyebrows too but not sure I'm brave enough to let my beloved loose on all my hairy bits.

Does your family have weird names for normal stuff ? For example, have you ever walked around a supermarket only to have your beloved shout across the aisles, 'Darling, do we need any bottom cheese?' No? Oh... it's just us then. Rod does love his bottom cheese which is in fact pont l'veque which, in fact, is approximately Bishop's bridge cheese and obvs is now known as either Bashing the Bishop cheese or, because of its disgusting smell when ripe, bottom cheese. I know.

Hot flushes are slightly better and improving daily which means I'm not dashing out and jumping in the pool at 3am any more. Rod has discovered me starkers, spread-eagled on the cold bathroom floor (usually only when the pool is green) and having a cold shower at weird times of the day and night in an effort to cool down. Seriously, the urge to undress in any company is always bubbling under the surface and is literally 30 seconds away 24/7 which must be a constant worry for any visitor.

Cooking is going well. Made chicken lasagne which was really good and chocolate-dipped strawberries. Made salmon fish cakes, carrot and chocolate cake, pies, pastries and pickled beetroot, fish soup, chilli con carne, pepper chicken, steak and loads of other stuff all of which my huge bottom can testify to. My whole day seems to revolve around 'what's for dinner tonight?' and I've even been googling recipes. Tomorrow is steak in pepper sauce with dauphinoise potatoes, poncy veg and the most time consuming starter I can think of. Making salted caramel ice cream which should hopefully take most of the day.

Have you noticed how little, insignificant things have become 'issues' which manifest into mountains? If I find tiny bits of coffee in the sugar bowl or dirty marks on the white hand towel in the bathroom or if he doesn't put a new loo roll on when he's finished the last one I will scream. Or, maybe just poor another vodka.

It's funny but the thing I really miss, most of all, is you lot, my friends who add so much to my life. See you all soon 💋

## Day: Run out of vodka so even considering cinzano.

I'm going to need a new dressing gown soon. Being a scabby cook/person generally, I seem to be perpetually covered in bits of bolognese sauce and/or soot from the fire, red wine, dirt, fabric softener, bleach, basically anything that can be squirted, dropped or splashed. My personal favourite is going to the loo in the middle of the night and managing to pee on the belt bit then touching it when I sleepily attempt to tie the belt when I've finished said pee.

Hair has become weird. Growing nicely, (apart from the copious amounts of grey) albeit a bit sticky-uppy. I look like medusa without the calming help of heated rollers and Mrs Slocombe with so I'll probably dye it purple and get some more cats.

Trying to cook interesting and different recipes has become the bain of my life. In fact, there is actually a website called 'What the F**k Shall I Cook for Dinner?' I shit you not. I'm googling things like twenty-seven million things to do with mince and what do other people have for supper? Made pizza last night which was good but that was then and this is now and I haven't got a Scooby for tonight. There are some profiteroles in the fridge and an opened tin of tuna so that should be OK together.

We have this group chat thingy with a questionable group of friends (Simon) and the lovely Gail suggested a quiz. So, after working out how to do the technical bit, (with excruciatingly painfully trying ineptly to follow Gail's instructions) the quiz started. Obvs we weren't prepared so my phone almost died and we had to go from kitchen to bedroom mid-quiz, find a pen, paper, top up drinks, get into bed, try not to flash unmentionable bits (always an issue with me) and answer the questions. We came second (I didn't add up the scores properly and Rod might be the tiniest bit bitter) so Simon won and didn't gloat at all. It was great fun and now we have mastered the whole Zoom thingy will hopefully not be so dim next time.

Had a trip to the DIY shop which was so exciting. New kitchen is well on its way with a lovely new floor, electrics and water and all the boring stuff done. Cannot wait for the units to be fitted and decorated with parrots and rainforest stuff. Consulted my interior designer, (Andrea, you are so polite. I could see you trying not to laugh when I said parrots) and we may go for a parrot and jungle wall frieze instead. Saw some amazing zebra print fabric that would look amazing in the new bathroom too...

The most marvellous thing about going out the other day was taking my bra off after actually getting dressed for a change! Not whilst we were out, obvs. Waited until we came home but I had really missed that feeling of whipping it off and letting it all hang out! Might actually put clothes on again soon.

Anyway, will leave you with that disturbing mental image and a fully clothed pic just to help cancel out any trauma you may now be suffering. See you all soon 💋

# Day: Some kind of nasty cheap booze from Lidl purportedly a Baileys thing but who really cares?

I seem to be spending more and more time either talking to myself or the cats. Either way, responses are somewhat lacking. Nigella just meows at me, the Ginger Pussy ignores me, Trevor eats and then buggers off and Duncan is so shallow it's untrue. All that leg rubbing and tail wagging then vanishes. Story of my life. Nigella does provide us with considerable entertainment and seems to think it's her right to come and wake us up in the morning (about 11ish) and demand her brunch.

It was bad enough living in the UK and the brats bothering us (we left the country to avoid them) but now the bloody cats are turning into right divas. Nigella thinks she owns the place - see below. Little shit. She takes up residence wherever she wants, including the cement mixer - not my first choice of bed but I don't expect anyone would bother me if I slept in there.

The fountain was looking a bit grimy this week so I turned it off and cleaned it out. Used the thingy that scoops the hibiscus from the pool and nearly fell in trying to empty the top tier of the fountain of jacaranda ferns. Killed the mozzies with bleach, put my hand in the middle tier and nearly puked on touching various bits of green gooey stuff that felt like bogey but it's all clean and shiny now. Pretentious? Moi? Absolutely darhlings.

Rodders has been hammering and banging away in the extension (no, not another euphemism) and my beautiful new kitchen now has a sink and hob and cupboards. We now have four kitchens (Rod gets bored) which is lovely but probably only encourages visitors which is really quite unpleasant. No, seriously, we love having people to stay. In fact, Rod is so enthusiastic about it I've left it until I'm on my way to the airport before mentioning that I might be picking up guests for a week in about ten minutes in order to contain his excitement.

First tomatoes of the year were harvested today. Chucked them in a rather garlicky pasta which was delish (just as well we're on lockdown) and hopefully in the next few days we'll have radish and lettuce. Shame bottles of Smirnoff don't grow in the garden but hey ho.

Had to engage with various brats this week and go through the whole 'I really miss you darlings' stuff. One of them is apparently going off to Australia to live which is quite marvellous. Coupled with another one that lives in Germany I'm doing rather well at getting shot of them. One is attempting to come here in the very near future but as long as it doesn't expect communication or interaction we should be fine.

Any interesting supper suggestions would be hugely appreciated as I'm spending ridiculous amounts of time googling recipes. In all honesty, I'm usually a bit tiddly by supper time so if you could ping recipes by about 1pm I would be exceedingly grateful. Ta.

Nigella marking her territory. I don't even like bloody cats.

# Day: 239 Days until Christmas

So I was in the kitchen listening to Miss Marple suss out the baddie whilst making puff pastry. Rodders wandered in with his 'is it beer o'clock?' face which obvs it is, always, but just needed affirmation from me so he doesn't feel like a total alcoholic. He found my favourite Plymouth Gin glass, found the vodka and splashed some in the glass. Anyhoo, you could have knocked me down with a feather! Is that how much (or should I say, little) you are supposed to put in a glass?? I thought it was chuck in two chunks of ice then half fill glass but apparently not which is clearly why the vodka bottle is always empty when I'm anywhere near it and seems bottomless when Rod does it. Wow - learn something new each day ...

Lovely to pick stuff from the garden for supper - lettuce, radish and tomatoes all tried and tested. Funnily enough, planting Smirnoff bottles hasn't worked but I live in hope.

Have you noticed how clean the air is? We have this fabulous view all the way to the sea from the garden. It's really quite marvellous but, over this last couple of weeks, the sky seems brighter, the sea is more visible and less hazy. I wonder what the animals and birds think about this lockdown business? I did ask The Ginger Pussy yesterday but as he's a) a cat and b) a Portuguese cat, the conversation was slightly one sided.

Caught up with the brats; well, you have to don't you? I've stopped asking them every day if they are OK. That was well beyond the realms of motherhood. A message once a week on our family WhatsApp is plenty - they'll expect to actually receive personal, individual texts soon and I'm really not that maternal. I mean, they are OK but very soon another one is headed off to distant shores so that eases the burden. Apart from the one that rings every day to see if I'm OK. Usually it's only because it wants to know how to cook something or what's my Amazon password but it seems like a nice kid so might actually let it come and see us once this is all over, as long as it doesn't stay too long ... or talk much.

So excited about the fabulous extension which is coming along in leaps and bounds. Rod is a clever sausage - bathroom in place, kitchen units, hob etc. Found parrot coloured tiles and paint and china parrots and little parrot door handles so it's going to look so understated and subtle. Really liking the idea of zebra or leopard print wallpaper for one wall in the bathroom. African Brothel is one theme I'm currently loving.

Right back at the beginning I mentioned making puff pastry - it was for some pastel de nata which are traditional Portuguese custard tarts. I've always believed life is too short to make puff pastry but these last few weeks have shown me that any activity is preferable to cleaning the bathroom yet again or dusting... again. The tarts came out beautifully - clearly felt an affinity somewhere along the lines.

Looks like things might be slowly going back to normal after next week. It's going to be weird not being drunk by 4pm and wearing a bra again. I trust my girlies can help with the first requirement but the second is slightly more compli-cated especially with the advent of the fabulous weather and my predilection for starkers swimming. Going to need some kind of industrial rigging to holster these droopy bazookas after probably only wearing a bra about three times in the last couple of months. And, on that glorious mental image, I shall leave you with a large V&T (Dawn measures) and hope to see you all soon.

Brat no. 5

## Day: My Name is Dawn and I'm an Alcoholic

I'm only joking (ish) but we are definitely drinking more or is it just over a longer period of time? We have switched to wine boxes which have so many added benefits. They don't run out nearly so often; the little tap on the front stands out nicely in red so when I'm really sloshed I can still find it; so much more environmentally friendly so we are, consequently, saving a polar bear at least twice a week.

My grey roots have miraculously vanished compliments of a €3 hair dye from Lidl. It was in the reduced section complete with purple label - the only hair dye left in the shop which, as I reached for it, I assumed would leave me looking like Lady GaGa (or possibly her much fatter grandmother). Luckily, it was a nondescript dark brown which I did consider asking Rod to apply for me but decided I wasn't that desperate. Did my eyebrows too, just like the hairdresser does. I looked like that artist Frida Kahlo - the mono brow look is not my finest so after considerable plucking I'm vaguely normal again.

Nail shops have opened again out here in Portugal so obvs was straight there for a repair job. Shallow moi? It's been quite refreshing to see all these posts about people cooking properly and going on nature walks and doing all this DIY and restoring stuff. I've been clicking like and love at all these smiling faces. But, girls, we know that all we really want to see is that the nail bar has Swarovski crystals and sparkly pink. Vaccines? World economy? Not quite up there in real life important stuff like glittery pink stiletto talons is it?

We've been having issues with the cats. Thought all this nonsense was behind us when we ran away from the kids and moved 1500 miles away. Apparently not. Little buggers have woken us up wanting to be fed, let out for a pee, had to stop them fighting, Rod had to speak to Terry about neglecting her kids (don't look at me) as she doesn't seem to want to spend any time with them. Personally, I think it's character building and mine loved boarding school.

Off to cook something incredible which will hopefully keep me busy until about 4 ish when it's just about acceptable to decide which wine glass to use today.

# Day: Homes Under the Hammer then Bargain Hunt.

It's been an eventful week as lockdowns go. Rod has had a haircut which is nice. It wasn't quite the whole removal of ear, nose and eyebrow hair too but he does look infinitely tidier and less like Brian May and more like George Clooney, ish.

One of the brats (Number 5 - its name will come to me) turned up at Lisbon airport so we toddled off to collect it. It seems quite nice so we let it into the house. And, it makes a reasonable G&T so obvs that helps. I've been trying my best to do all the maternal stuff. We took it for a walk in the park and to the swings. It pointed out that as it's twenty-five maybe we could look for alternatives. Spoilt brat. Never satisfied. Today we took it to Loule Rugby Club as it's quite a reasonable player. I thought I might offer to help with the first 15 there - you know; run on (well, lollop really) with a sponge and mop those hunky brows. I'm good like that.

Played Gin Rummy last night. Rod won the first game and only gloated slightly - making the loser sign at me was so child-ish. His behaviour deteriorated when I won the next round - he called me the 'c' word which is not particularly friendly but I suppose cleaning the loo with his toothbrush was possibly an over- reaction.

One of the other brats has this ridiculous dog. It (the dog, not the brat) thinks it's a Dobermann and not a Chihuahua.

Found the most shamazeballs parrot 🦜 picture to go in the

new kitchen. Well, it's more of a 'Bloody Nora! What the hell is that??' than a parrot picture. A whole parrot wall in fact. I did look at understated and subtle but it brought me out in a rash so decided against it. I do wonder sometimes why I can't be happy with an IKEA kitchen and instead say things to Rod like 'can we have that in bright red?' or 'leopard print and gold would look so much better.' I think it's my inner brothel trying to escape.

Duncan the daddy cat has buggered off. Bloody typical. He's had his wicked way with Terry, kittens arrived and he can't stick around to help bring the kids up. Nigella and Terry have been terrorised by the Ginger Pussy. He chased Nigella up a tree and as he's too fat to get up there himself, (I know the feeling) had to wait until GP finally gave up and wandered off. Nigella has taken to sunbathing. Why don't our cats catch mice like normal cats? Oh no. Much easier to leave Samuel Whiskers (our resident rat) to live behind the bar and eat the cat food provided. Can't help feeling this relationship is slightly one sided.

On that note I need to leave you as Rod is choosing a CD to play whilst we have dinner. Left unsupervised it will either be Little Mix or Chas & Dave which wouldn't be my first choice.

# Day: Yet Another Trip to the Bottle Bank

Momentous day yesterday - the first swim (and wee obvs) of the summer in the pool. I'm a bit like the Great Wall of China - visible from the international space station as it orbits the Earth. That tsunami/earthquake was only me breast stroking the way middle aged women do - head up trying not to splash hair and make-up.

Number 5 is still here. It doesn't stop eating - says you need cake to warm your tummy up before breakfast. It's unpacked and is talking about decorating it's bedroom. We really thought that moving countries and being 1500 miles away might have stopped this kind of unpleasantness but the brats have this inbuilt homing device and insist on communication and actual real life contact. Apparently, according to Google, it's because I'm its mother but I can't see the connection myself.

I found a three-thousand piece jigsaw in the cupboard which has cheered Rodders up no end. He's doing the edges and Number 5 is doing a middle bit. My role in this activity seems to be the lady (lady? bit of a stretch) that turns the pieces over to the picture side. Personally, I feel my talents aren't being fully utilised.

Extension is coming along splendidly. Rod is a clever bunny at all that building stuff. He's stopped rolling his eyes at me every time I mention parrots and painting walls bright green and just says yes dear. Went out today looking for curtains - I'm thinking Palace of Versailles ish which should fit in well with the tiny little minute chandeliers and gold cherubs. I do like to keep things subtle.

My technical skills are pretty rubbish - on a par with an ant - but I did manage to make my avatar. Avatar Dawn is slightly less rotund than me but what's a minuscule bit of poetic licence between friends? The outfits available aren't great either - I was hoping for something a bit more appropriate as I'm not so much Marks & Spencer but more Morticia/Nell Gwynn. Hopefully the powers that be will add to the selection and I can revise the outfit soon - do you think I could email them and suggest something a tad more dominatrix?

It's such a boiley hot day I'm off to displace another couple of tons of water. It's fine - Green Peace know it's only me. Stay safe kids, mucho love ♥

## Day: Freedom! (ish)

Absolutely marvellous weather after the rain so my angel conscience is telling me to weed the garden whilst the devil bit (considerably larger) is screaming, pour large V&T and swim or blob out on a sun lounger. The fact we now could do with a goat to sort the garden out reveals exactly which path I followed (as per usual).

No 5 made tea this morning and delivered it to us in bed. Nice cup of Earl Grey, offered to make breakfast too. *Homes Under the Hammer* had only just started so we politely declined but told it to come back after *Bargain Hunt*. Decided No 5 needed a name so 'Rose' seems appropriate after the maid in *Upstairs Downstairs* in an attempt to encourage this recent interest in housework it seems to have discovered. Anyway, Rose is easier to remember than it's real name. I came up with that one nearly twenty-six years ago so how am I expected to remember?

Ventured out into the real world yesterday and had a coffee (wine) with the lovely Penny in Loule. It was a bank holiday here yesterday - apparently it was the Spinach Festival... yep, I shit you not. Wasn't sure how that actually manifests itself but it's a day off so it's all good.

We've been watching a dreadful series on Prime - *The Last Ship*. Acting leaves a great deal to be desired but the concept is interesting and so relevant to today's situation. The lead character looks like Eagle Eyes Action Man and is an all-American hero and thoroughly decent chap who obvs saves the world. In fact, we are so in awe of the ship's Captain, Rod decided to name our luxury, ocean-going yacht after Action Man's ship, the Nathan James, which is currently in dry dock pending repairs - need the Chinese shop to re-open so we can buy a puncture repair kit.

Today is No 4's birthday (I have this reminder thing in my phone - don't get excited, it wasn't my maternal instinct kicking in). We phoned and I sang happy birthday to it which was nice as it had a lovely hangover and was in bed eating Pringles. Happy happy birthday my beautiful smelly witch 🧹. Mama loves you.

Brat no.4

## Day: Is it Christmas yet?

Girls, I have a cucumber tree. Yep, and when you pick one, another one is ready. You can grow them as little or BIG as you like. It's really quite marvellous. Hoping the butternut squash and the courgettes will be ready soon....

Apart from that we've had an uneventful week. The voodoo cat is back. The Ginger Pussy makes signs with the chicken bones once she's stripped them - feels like she's casting a spell on us which is a bit weird but that cat is quite unpleasant. She has the biggest dangly thingys (she's a chap) and chases the other cats up trees, eats all the food then buggers off. Typical bloke.

Finally finished watching the awful series, *The Last Ship*. It was terrible but compulsive at the same time. You know those dreadful exaggerated facial expressions actors pull? Like Nikki the pathologist in Silent Witness - she has this permanently perplexed expression and I'm sure it's why she's taken to Botox. All those frown lines just from over-acting. Well, the actors in *The Last Ship* do it too, obvs when they aren't busy saving the world.

We've moved on to *Vikings* which fulfils Rod's requirements; shagging, gun fights and car chases. Obvs you have to substitute the gun fight with axes and bows and arrows and the car chase for galloping across hills and things or longship chases but you know what I mean.

Put some toys in the pool for Brat No. 5 to play with. It's

explained that at twenty-five-and-three quarters perhaps a blow up dinosaur called Dylan is a wee bit young. So ungrateful. Apparently I should know what twenty-five-and-three-quarter-year-olds like doing as it's my fifth one to reach that age. I explained that the whole maternal thing is not really my thing and I didn't take much notice. It wasn't impressed.

Rodney is still beavering away in the extension. He's doing absolutely splendidly and I can't wait to move into our new bedroom. Have been looking at ideas on Pinterest although there are surprisingly few offerings under 'Leopard print, bling, Palace of Versailles, harlot' so I'm having to improvise. Found a chandelier for the kitchen - vital - and seen the most amazing mirror with disco lights for the bathroom. Subtle and elegant.

No. 5 has just bunged a dye on my hair so I'm sitting here, typing this drivel, slowly cooking. I'm aiming for the Elizabeth Taylor look but have a feeling it's going to be more Dracula-ish. We can go to the hairdressers now but I really do not want to sit there with a mask on for over an hour (compulsory here) so I'll stick to this Lidl's own brand dye which I'm sure will be incredible. And, having your ears, cheeks and neck dyed is included for free when No. 5 does it. Which is nice.

Prawn fried rice for dinner tonight. I've already prepped the prawns, washed all the poo out which No.5 nearly gagged over. Snowflake. I'm going to make it gut the sardines tomorrow - that should make it leave home!

The memories thingy reminded me that it's four years since I was diagnosed with breast cancer. It's been all change since then but, only the good die young so obvs I'm still here to tell the tale. I'm posting this awful picture because this is the reality of cancer. I'm asking every one of you to check your boobies, book an overdue smear test or have a thorough investigation of your dinkle and dangly bits (that'll be the chaps) because you never know.

So darhlings, have the grooviest of weekends and stay safe. Ooo, it's V&T o'clock...

Rod and me

# Day: It's life Jim, but not as we know it!

I was told off this week. Actually, you wouldn't be surprised to know that me being told off is a fairly regular occurrence. Popped to the shopping centre in search of suitable happy birthday presents for Rodders. Brat no.5 wanted a rummage in Primani (as they always do) and in true middle aged menopausal woman form, I needed the loo. Off I went and was informed rather forcefully that I was attempting to exit using the entrance. The lady told me to go out of the other doors on the other side of the shop. I said, really? You want me to walk all the way around, avoiding no one at all? Obviously I told her not to be so ridiculous and didn't she know who I was? I certainly wasn't about to queue up to go back into the shop! At least 50 people queuing - who needs cheap knickers that badly?? Madness! She was not a happy bunny but it's all so contradictory and daft - you have to wear your mask to go into the shopping centre but take it off when you sit at the indoor cafes...

Anyway, no. 5 seemed happy with its purchases. I did ask it if it wanted to play in the playground or have an ice cream but it just scowled at me and asked if I'd ever been to any parenting classes or knew what a maternal instinct was. I had to google but still don't understand.

Rod has been a poorly sausage - hurt his back (swinging from the chandelier again) - so his birthday celebrations were somewhat subdued as he was barely able to stand. We sang happy birthday to him (did you think you heard screaming hyenas on Wednesday?) and he loved his pressies. I cooked his special birthday dinner of prawn cocktails followed by steak and chips. All we needed was Black Forest gateaux for our retro 70's supper! His favourite cake, carrot and chocolate, a few games of gin rummy accompanied by a glass or two of vino and off to bed with *Vikings*. Rod can't wait to play with his new toys and I can't wait for more chandelier swinging.

My magic potion seems to be taking effect slightly earlier than usual - have you ever tried finding a royal flush whilst having the munchies and trying to empty a dishwasher into the fridge to make the cutlery happy? Pop it on your to-do list for a giggle.

Had a socially distanced (ish) Writing Group meeting which was fabulous. Things are slowly becoming normal again but with a huge elephant in the room - the virus stuff is everywhere and trying to find a balance between not dying and having a life is tricky. Not keen on popping my clogs just yet so trying to maintain a yin and yang. Besides, I so don't want to expire from a virus with loads of other people. Looking for something considerably more spectacular such as paragliding from the moon or being eaten by an albino killer whale. If it doesn't make News at Ten I will be devastated.

Anyway, leaving you with this birthday pic of us, like the Queen does. Mucho kisses 💋

# Day: You Really Couldn't Make This Shit Up

As I lay in bed last night listening to Rodders snoring, (after watching three episodes of *Vikings* which may account for his wiggling about in his sleep last night - probably dreaming of a bit of rampaging and pillaging whilst shouting Valhalla) it occurred to me that Friday nights have changed.

At 1am I was googling 'what are the things on top of my onions?' and 'what can I make with millions of butternut squashes?' which is all very informative but not particularly rock and roll. Brat No. 5 just asked if I wanted a vodka and tonic but I declined in favour of a mint tea. That's so wrong on so many levels and I promise to change.

Rod has been a poorly sausage but after my tender loving care he's on the mend. Actually, I think it was possibly the visits to the osteopath which have cured him but I'm happy to take the credit. Anyone examining our bed would easily be able to ascertain exactly what I have cooked over the last week from the blobs and splodges of bolognaise sauce, soup (I had to sniff that one - it was carrot and beetroot but looked like baby poo) and a bit of squished burger. The red wine stains were me - a combination of several glasses of vino, my magic potion cannabis oil and a particularly rude scene on *Vikings*. I've changed the bed and thankfully we are on the last season of *Vikings*.

On Wednesday I abandoned Rod and the brat in favour

of a lovely night out with two super ladies, Anne and Lesley. Had to do a bit of prep obvs; mustachios issues and hairy legs too. After having chemo and being a baldilocks my hairy bits haven't grown back quite how I'd like them too. I mean, why have I now got a hairy face and why didn't it all grow back on my head instead of leaving baldy patches which have to be hidden with comb-overs??

Anyway, it was so good to go out for an Indian, (to eat, not to go and buy an Indian because that's just not cricket these days) have a chat and eat out. Dinner was fabulous - that place in Vilamoura opposite the Stableford Bar - what smashing people! Leslie is definitely not destined for upstairs as she's far too naughty and wicked (takes one to know one) but Anne will absolutely be on the up escalator. It was very quiet and so few people about which is so sad to see but hopefully with lots of caution, life will slowly become easier. I wouldn't say back to normal because that's not really a word I (or the vast majority of my friends) have much in common with.

Vomit alert - I won't post a pic of my beloved and I today (no make up, menopausal spots and no bra) but will leave you with some pics of our beautiful flowers. Last year for our anniversary Rod bought me seven rose bushes - seventh Anniversary, the itchy one. We haven't murdered each other yet and he still calls me darling (occasionally) so today this red rose bloomed and is absolutely beautiful. So, on that note I will say laters alligators. Going to send the maid (no. 5) to peel the spuds for dinner whilst I pour another V&T and have a bath because I smell. Lots of love kids and be kind ♥

## Day: Is Vodka Acceptable for Breakfast? Asking for a Friend.

I've turned into one of those old women who walk around the garden, talking to myself, showing far too much enthusiasm for carrots, cucumbers, courgettes and aubergines (stop that you filthy beasts). I'm not actually talking to myself - just mumbling inane comments to the vegetables as I pull out weeds and pick stuff - 'ooo! Those radishes need thinning out' and 'I'll just pick those tomatoes and maybe you need some leaves tweaked off' which is incredibly boring. I'd quite like to emulate Charlie Dimmock but have a feeling I'm more Percy Thrower.

I've become a bit obsessed with painting anything that stands still. Our ancient wrought iron table and chairs are now gleaming and white. Brat no. 5 helped out yesterday which was nice but the quantity of paint which was applied to the two old garden benches seems to be significantly less than the quantity of paint on its hair, hands and feet. Div.

In other news, I may have crashed the car slightly. Well, I say crashed, but it was just a tiny reversing kind of bollard smashed lights kind of thing. I've never been a fan of reversing. There was that hearse incident, then Brat No.5's bright yellow car which I didn't see ... Anyhooo, it's not my fault I'm easily distracted.

Finally had a haircut (four months' worth) and I must say,

despite the fact that young Simone doesn't speak English and my Portuguese is limited to important words like vino and vodka (ooooo - it's the same! How splendid!) the whole experience was a resounding success. I no longer resemble Medusa but more one of those old ladies you see having cut price OAP afternoon tea after playing bingo.

Treated myself to some new diamond earrings from the Chinese shop - so pleased these amazing places are open again. If ever you need pink plastic roses or a silver diamanté nodding Buddha let me know and I'll point you in the right direction.

The extension is nearly finished - shutters went up yesterday and we are moving into our new bedroom tomorrow. It will take a bit of acclimatising - you know that middle of the night drunk feeling when you need the loo and you're staying in an hotel or someone else's house and end up peeing in the sitting room? That. So, wish me luck.

Enough of my drivel, you will be so grateful to hear, as it's time to drag myself out of bed, make my beloveds porridge, look longingly at the Lidl's own brand vodka (Rachmaninov - €6), open the fridge and decide what to cook for dinner tonight.

Leaving you with our view and my butternut squashes because trust me, they are far more attractive than me on a Sunday morning. Have a groovy one kids - mwah 🌑

*Day: I have no idea what I'm allowed to call things these days so will just say Peace Man and obvs Woman and everyone in between, even that American woman who married a tree.*

Today children, we are going to talk about spaghetti bolognaise, amongst other things. How can you argue about spag bol and how does a mumsie Facebook cooking page utilised by middle class, Archers listening, G&T slurping, peri-menopausal women degenerate into Felicity calling Caroline an 'uneducated c**t' whilst Caroline's friend Camilla replies with 'Oh! I say! Do f**k orf' ???

There I was scrolling through my recipe pages thinking, what the 'kin 'ell am I going to cook for dinner tonight? when I stumbled across a post saying '37,000 Things to do with a Pound of Mince.' Felicity's pic of spag bol looked well dodgy but hey ho, each to their own. Maybe these gals have run out of gin and the private schools aren't opening until September (such a drag darhling - I know mine used to break up last week of bloody June - purgatory). But, wow, Cheltenham Ladies College would be shuddering or possibly even fainting at the language! It all stemmed from Caroline telling Felicity that didn't she know carrots were not supposed to be added to spag bol - that was a common mistake. Then it was who are you calling common etc.

and well the rest has given me plenty of material for my next fish-wife outburst, when I do the thing properly and throw stuff at Rod because he's left the top off the toothpaste or something.

Personally, I'm with Felicity. When the brats were little, I used to put mushrooms, carrots, broccoli, any veg I had, into a blender and chuck it in the mix then obvs lied to them when they asked if there were mushrooms. Sorry kids.

Now that we have an upstairs, we have the issue of stuff that downstairs needing to be upstairs and the upstairs stuff needing to go down. Ladies, you know what I mean - that sock, book, specs, dirty washing, clean washing... Anyway, we know don't we? We just know what needs to go where. Men and brats have absolutely no comprehension at all and even think they are being helpful when they scoop it all up and bring it down or up. They are rubbish. And sooooo annoying. How can you not know where I had intended the car keys and an apple and a biro and €4 in shrapnel to go?

Terry the cat had two kittens! We finally saw them and, because in these somewhat excitable times, we are very proud to announce one is ginger and the other black and white! Hopefully that won't upset/offend anyone and we promise to love them all the same, even the ginger one.

OMG!! I grew the most amazing carrot! I've called him Dennis because he looks like a Darlek. We have eaten him now, with hummus - lovely, but, his memory will live on.

I'll show you our beautiful upstairs once I've done some housework because no one wants to see Rod's discarded knickers or my bleach stained Primani leggings decorating the sofa.

Have a wonderful day and be kind to one another and yourselves. Mucho love 🖤

# Day: Furry Grandparents!

The stork has been to see us and left two little bundles of joy on the doorstep! Well, I say bundles of joy when in fact I mean two more demanding little noise machines who poo in the flower beds. Terry the mummy cat has finally introduced her kittens to us. There's a black one we've called Peter after a delightful chap some of our chums in Folkestone may well know. He's a gentleman from overseas who is frequently to be found propping up the bar at The Park Inn. Seemed appropriate. The other ginger one has been lumbered with the rather wonderful moniker, Menelaus but we'll probably call it Menny for short. Aren't we clever producing a ginge and a black one - none of that white supremacy rubbish here which is all part of the reason for allowing them to self-identify their genders when they feel ready because we're modern progressive people embracing rainbows and fluffy bunnies.

In other news, I've had toothache. Well, let's just rewind. It wasn't just toothache - it was off the bloody scale, moaning, whining, whinging and girly foot stamping ouchiness. And, it actually turned out not to be tooth ache but a dislocated jaw, (no, Rod did not finally thump me - not that anyone would blame him let's face it). Relocation was fun - not. I was brave; the osteopath had fingers in my delicate bouche and under my (slightly hairy I noticed afterwards) chin. Inhale he said, then came the ex-hale and I thought he'd pulled my bloody head off but blimey! It worked! I loved it so much that I went back and had another session. It was a bit of a chain from chemo leading to a bone spur on my jaw, dislodging the teeth and causing dislocation. Painkillers and anti-inflammatory sweeties have kept me in zip a dee doo dah land all week so every cloud.

Anyway, why can't brats load dishwashers? I'm not being ungrateful - just mystified. Seriously, every time no. 5 puts stuff in the dishwasher it looks like they've just been bunged in where the little bugger dropped them. It watched me unload all its handiwork and mumbled stuff like, dunno why I bovver, as I tutted and rearranged. Apparently it's because we, us old people, played Tetris when we were not quite so prehistoric whilst they are much more sophisticated with Assassins Creed and the other one where they shoot people from stolen police cars. Really? Is that what my kids were doing? Anyway, we've agreed no.5 can rinse and stack on the bench and I'll load. On the plus side, it can make a decent G&T so I'll obvs forgive it.

Talking of which, I've become teetotal. Well, let's just analyse that statement. I've not had a drink for over a week due to being loaded up with drugs and I'm not sure that having several large vodka's or half a wine box on board would improve matters. I'm even down to my pre-lockdown weight of 5XL which is great news.

Leaving you with Terry, Menelaus and Peter and some cupcakes I made this week because we're only doing happy stuff today. Have the most marvellous weekend kids - do unto others and all that jazz. Mwah 💋

# Day: Puke Alert – you may well need a sick bucket.

Oooooo, where shall I start? OK, do you remember the cucumber tree? Well, now I have a lettuce tree. Didn't mean to grow a lettuce tree to be fair - just the lettuce bit would have been enough but I'm not really, (well at all let's face it) a by halves kind of girl. So, we have this beautiful green thing that's a cross between salad and Christmas. Actually, maybe we'll keep it going until then and shove some fairy lights on it and bob's your uncle. I actually forgot to pick it. Well, I say forgot but we did have enough lettuce in the fridge to have kept Peter Rabbit's great-grandchildren fed three meals a day for life and Mr McGregor wouldn't have put them anywhere near that pie. It was like a bloody Amazonian rainforest in the fridge so thought it wouldn't hurt to leave just one doing its' thing. That the baby lettuce seedling is now a thing, it needs a name. I'm thinking Larry sounds good. A sort of 'let us (pardon the pun) pop down the pub for a mineral water' kind of name. It's got quite a ring to it - bit of salad cream and Larry the Lettuce will be well on his way.

Rod's romantic side has really excelled this week. There I was, listening to an Archers Omnibus, weeding the garden, yanking out the scraggy old mint tangling my pretty pink roses. Something attacked me! Well, alright, it was just a plant thing where my gloves finished but I was stung to buggery and blotchy and swollen and sooooo itchy I even went to bed with wet tea towels wrapped around my arms! Anyhoooo, my beloved came home the other day with 5 litres of cleaning stuff for the pool and the sexiest gardening gloves ever! To be honest, they do actually look more like something a dominatrix might keep in her bedside drawer as opposed to being just right for weeding flower beds but, I was so overwhelmed with Rod's display of love and devotion, bless him.

Terry the mummy cat has been tirelessly feeding her demanding off-spring. Peter seems slightly more adventurous than Menelaus but let's face it, Menelaus is probably still coming to terms with its name and having counselling. We'll have their dangly bits or noonies dealt with ASAP we can catch all of them. Nigella, the other cat who seems to have adopted us, has taken to sleeping on the sofa in our bedroom or on the bed - cheeky bugger. And, she can talk - I shit you not! We woke up the other morning and Rod thought Brat No.5 was calling me and all I could hear was 'muumm'! which obvs I ignore at every opportunity, especially before coffee, but it was Nigella! We moved countries to escape the kids (true story - soz kids) only to have replaced brats with equally demanding talking fluff balls. So unfair. I don't even like cats. I do sometimes wish I did have that maternal instinct thing then look at photos of all six of the brats together, remember the logistics of managing riding lessons, rugby matches, piano lessons, trampolining and a birthday party all at 3pm on a Sunday afternoon and pray I don't end up with about 27 grandchildren. I'll move to Siberia or somewhere if they start turning up with kids and expecting me to babysit or something equally as horrible (for the kid - not me).

Anyway, enough of my baloney. Have a marvellous weekend, be happy and safe and smile. Be kind. Lots of love 🖤

Duncan the cat

# Day: Cat Woman without the black sexy outfit because that would just look gross on me.

An incredibly brave mosquito bit me on the bottom last night. I don't suppose it survived after a swig of my blood which, despite my new teetotal status, is probably a) still a bit radioactive from my daily boobie zapping three years ago and, b) about 90% Smirnoff. Hopefully, if he did live to tell the tale, he's gone home to his mates and told them to a) avoid the human with the big wobbly bottom and, b) he's suffering the hangover from hell this morning.

Nigella the cat has taken to giving me dirty looks - see below. Seriously, could a cat look more pissed off if it tried? Sent Rod the photo of Nigella 'helping' with his 3000 piece jigsaw - response isn't printable. Woke up to find Nigella on the end of the bed, giving me daggers, I apologised, she moved to the sofa and went back to sleep. If she could speak, I think her favourite expression would be 'ffs! Who even are you and what are you doing in my house?' I don't even like cats.

Had a re-think of the whole parrot thing for the new kitchen and have decided to go with fish instead. Chiefly because we have so many fish things we've collected. It started with Gilbert - a big blue fish vase thing Rod called Gilbert Poisson and it all snow-balled from there. Brian the Fish was next and the most recent one is a dish called Maureen - we always name them after the people we buy them from which is a bit weird but saves any arguments. So, while Rod's been away, I may have rearranged the house just a tiny bit. The new kitchen looks fab with all the fishy stuff everywhere and I really do think the parrots will be happier in the big kitchen downstairs. A psychiatrist would have a field day with us....

I've become a bit addicted to gardening but it would be helpful if I was better at it. Planted loads of stuff which I thought were aubergines and courgettes but now they've grown it transpires that they are in fact watermelons and butternut squashes. Moussaka is possibly going to taste slightly strange but I tried. Actually, I've become really housewifely and prepared tonight's dinner last night. Chucked stuff in the slow cooker to be more accurate but the tomatoes, onions and peppers all came from the garden and taste fabulous. Hopefully managed to wash off all the pee-bugs, caterpillars and soil but after eight hours in a slow cooker I don't suppose anyone will notice. Actually, it's just me and Number 5 for the next week-ish so the extra bits will make it go further and save me cooking tomorrow night.

I promise to continue this whole doing housework thing and will take some photos of Gilbert and Brian, the new kitchen and our rather spectacular new bedroom once I've hoovered up the monkey nut bits - never ever eating nuts in bed again - and made the bed. Might have to wait until I change it again for the once a week making the bed ceremony.

Here's Nigella with her 'Ffs' face on. Look carefully - there is a cat sprawled over the jigsaw!!

Love and kisses kids and be nice to each other ♥💋

# Day: If I have a shower will it all have been a dream?

Haven't had a drink now (alcofrolic obvs) for four whole weeks which sadly has repercussions for Smirnoff who are on the brink of bankruptcy but, on the plus side, my bottom had shrunk just a tiny bit! Morphine and vodka can be a bit of a dodgy old mix so thought I'd better knock the booze on the head for a while. Who knew I could be sooooo sensible and grown up? It was a shock to me so you lot must be positively aghast! Anyway, skin is definitely better - my old lady spots have cleared up and I no longer resemble Red Beard the Pirate. Result!

We've been out a few times now which is great - feels very different here without all the tourists. We are blessed with fabulous weather and being able to sit outside virtually every day which feels safer than being stuck indoors with lots of sweaty/smelly bodies so hopefully the economy here will cope. We all wear our masks and adhere to the rules which is probably just as well or the armed police would be slightly cheesed off. Funnily enough, there haven't been any statues removed or protests here....

You know how subtle and modest I am? Well, we thought it was time the fountain had a bit of a makeover and it now looks marvellous darlings! I constantly want to tiddle when it's tinkling away but that might just be an old woman thing?

I'm doing fabulously at this growing stuff - I've got a

lurverly pair of watermelons! Sent Brat No.5 out with a bowl last night to pick whatever was ready and it came back with cherry tomatoes, peppers and chillies. Also have some scotch bonnets ready so I'm thinking a blow-your-head-off curry ? Better than colonic irrigation too!

My beloved has toodled orf to Blighty for a few days so I'm taking advantage and being a) lazy b) catching up with girl friends and c) watching crap on the telly he doesn't like. Has anyone seen 'The Cry'? It's fantastic and has massive overtones of the McCanns - worth a watch.

No.5 is still here. It seems to like it - can't understand how anyone would want to live with me but there's no accounting for taste. If anyone needs a house sitter, dog walker, baby sitter etc. please let me know because I'd quite it to clear off and stop laughing at my Neil Diamond sing a long sessions and it's not polite to tell your mother it's time for a care home just because I put the mayonnaise in the dishwasher or the washing in the oven. Horrible brat.

Leaving you with a modest pic of me, not posing at all, and, the fruits of my labours. Have a wonderful weekend kids, lots of love 🖤

# Day: What even is an unopened bottle of vodka?

Having a bit of a breakdown as another brat wants to come and see us/stay for a 'bit' and, bring a 'friend.' To be fair, No.3 is relatively normal and I even quite like it so as long as it doesn't expect too much in the way of communication and/or interaction we should be fine.

Bloody cats are eating a ridiculous amount and have become fussy, noisy, pooing in the flowers little gits. Typical men in fact. It transpires that Peter and Menelaus have tiny little furry gentleman's bits and bobs so hopefully the pitter patter of even more tiny feet is on hold for now. They have become quite bold, venturing into the kitchen and giving us daggers when we dare to leave the food bowl empty. Terry, their mum, is quite partial to fresh fish but, only if it's cooked. She turned her nose up at the dorada heads but ate the cooked leftovers. I chucked the heads in the microwave and the little bugger devoured the lot.

Still not drinking, I shit you not! Not a drop of anything alcoholic has passed my lips which is not only proving wonderful for my skin, slowly losing weight too. I do actually have one spot on the side of my nose which is why the gruesome photo I've posted is from the spot-free side. It's a proper witch-spot - not a huge surprise really.

Anyway, I finally made the bed. Only because my beloved came home and I had to make it look like I had actually been all housewifely rather than slatternly for the last two weeks. Not sure Rod was convinced but he seemed pleased to see me... or maybe he just wanted a lift home from the airport? Here are a few photos of our subtle and understated new bedroom. As you can see it's all very tasteful and the bar is a very sophisticated finishing touch. Not sure if the chandeliers are big enough but we can always add some more dangly, shiny bits.

Had lunch at the Marina today - it was nice but really just posh KFC. We chose a new yacht then decided not to bother after all because staff are so hard to find these days so we'll stick to the dingy in the pool at home.

Here's a weird grinning un-spotty picture of us! Love to you all.

Brat no. 2 and mummy

## Day: I blame it all on the aliens who built the pyramids.

I babysat for this kid this week. I know - how irresponsible of its mother! Went quite well really - kid falls into the 'tolerable' category as opposed to 'put it on eBay' so that was a bonus. I was nice to it; threats of old lady sloppy kisses usually make kids behave perfectly. It wasn't impressed with the homework I made it do but, for every correct spelling, it was allowed a sweet so economics and bribery were also themes we explored. Kid lived to tell the tale and doesn't hate me so I'll count that as a maternal gold star.

Isn't it lovely when an old face pops up on a Facebook group ? I noticed a familiar name on our old school group, my physics teacher - Mr Paine. He was a jolly nice chap and despite his best efforts, I was never really much good but, my big brother Tim, one year above me, was. Now, the set homeworks were the same each year for the physics 'O' level course so obvs I copied Tim's homework. He made me do his chores and make him coffee and stuff - horrible boy. Anyway, I confessed to the lovely Mr Paine who ordered me straight into detention but maybe now I'm 53 and not 14 it's possibly a bit late. I scraped a C grade and luckily have never had cause to use a Bunsen burner or potassium permanganate since leaving school but definitely feel better for my confession.

Cats have finally decided we are no longer scary monsters which is nice. Terry, Peter and Menelaus have stopped pooing in the flower beds which is great but now seem to favour the carrots which I discovered when I thought it would be a good idea to make a carrot and butternut squash soup this week. Gardening is all fun and games until you pull up a handful of poo along with your onions. And, let's talk about Nigella. Nigella has become our little shadow and I cannot believe I've fallen for this whole cat take-over of our lives. I have even placed a really soft squidgy blanket on the sofa for Nigella to sleep on. I don't even like cats.

Today is our living in paradise anniversary! Four years ago we bought our beautiful home here in Loule. It's seen loads of changes and renovations, we've had some fabulous guests, parties, memories and made some wonderful friends. It became my haven during such a dreadful time whilst I was so ill, (nearly dead ill - I'd ask for a refund on the voodoo doll whoever that was - defo faulty) and Rod's awesome skills in making our beautiful home the wonderful, bit weird, place it is today. (And my carrot growing skills obvs). We love our life here and hope for many more years to come. Well, until we can't do the stairs and pee ourselves and dribble and stuff.

Have a wonderful day darlings, lots of love from the Strawberries 🖤🍓

# Day: I think it may be time to shout my safe word!

Had an eventful week which was juxtaposed between pickled onions and Bridget Jones knickers. There is rather a great deal squeezed into the middle so I'll go through it in vaguely chronological order for good form.

This bother with my delicate and tiny gob came to a painful crescendo on Monday when a lump the size of a golf ball popped out under my chin. We called it Gordon and then added Larry as a middle name, as one does. Anyway, Gazza and I popped off to the hospital whereupon I was systematically prodded and poked, examined and ultra-sounded, blood tested (not a drop of alcohol!!) then dripped magic potions of various kinds. Anyhoooo, more stuff of the same ilk followed the next day and Gordon seems to be pushing off. I no longer resemble a lop-sided Frankensteinean monster - it just looks like a blob of blobby stuff which is shrinking daily. Which leads me neatly on to pickled onions.

I am sooooo proud of managing to grow enough onions to keep Sarson's shares afloat! Dunno who's going to eat the jars of pickled onions now gracing the pantry because Rod doesn't like them and snogging (😷) will obvs be out of the question if I eat any. It's the thought that counts. Apparently, No. 3, who is due to make an appearance in the not too distant future, likes them - I just hope its considerably better half does too or the breath and poppy bottom issues may well impact on the length of stay.

Now for the quite magnificent knickers - four pairs max at any one time on the line. The best M&S Bridget Jones' needed to be utilised for the benefit of the medical staff. Not that they were remotely interested in looking in the vicinity but it's polite to be prepared. I'm at the stage in life where all that lacy frippery is far too much like hard work and quite unnecessary - cup of tea and Netflix is much more agreeable to slightly plump, middle aged, menopausal women. No. 5 hammered the last nail into the coffin in fact. It laughed as I put the washing out and said 'blimey! Size of those! Whose are those?' Div. Hardly going to be Rod's now are they? It's flight is booked.

Made the most shamazeballs bread today to go with French onion soup - rosemary, garlic and onion. This gardening thing is becoming an obsession. I've even started saving seeds and putting them in little jars with labels. I shit you not - I'm a reincarnation of Percy Thrower with boobs. Boob.

Nigella has become even more demanding than No.5. She sat on the middle of the rug this morning and moaned at us. If she could speak it would be along the lines of 'you lazy gits - get up and feed me slaves.' I really don't like cats.

Happy weekend kids. Be kind and smile. Obvs not if you're wearing a mask though because that would be silly. Love.

# Day: Purple Lizards

Don't tell on me but I've just nicked a load of figs from our neighbour's tree. I'll make some jam with them tomorrow and be all domesticated. I've even been saving jars especially. I wonder exactly when this metamorphosis happens in women? What triggers wanting to grow tomatoes and watch *The Antiques Roadshow* with a cup of tea in preference to reading articles about bonking in Cosmopolitan and saying yes to vodka shots on a school night?

This teetotal thing is still going splendidly. It's not even a thing any more - just a bit boring drinking water constantly. But, boring is good when it means my bottom has gone from mountainous to hillocks. Never ever in a million years thought I'd stop influencing Smirnoff's share prices but it's all fun and games until you wake up without a hangover and realise there is this day called 'Sunday.'

We've decided to investigate all these marvellous conspiracy theories. Keeping an open mind about it all, including the stuff about the pyramids being power sources for UFO's to refuel - a sort of service station for ET to pop in and buy a Mars bar and a coffee when he's had a long day along with some diesel, well, not diesel more this ray of power stuff that's beamed up from the pyramid. You can tell we've run out of stuff to watch on Netflix.

I have two beautiful new raised planter beds in the garden.

Rod has worked so hard making them for me to grow stuff for when I'm really old and can't bend over. So thoughtful. This time when I plant things I'm going to translate the packets and seedlings properly in an effort to avoid being inundated with peppers and butternut squash because there is a limit to my creativity with just two veggies.

The cats have become very lazy and moan if they have to actually take the chicken off the bone themselves. The look of disdain Nigella gave me today when offered a bowl of chicken wings was really quite unpleasant. She took her revenge by pooing in the petunias whilst ignoring my shouts of 'bugger off you little sod.' Reminds me of six brats I know...

Talking of brats, number five has returned to England. We may well move in case it decides to return! Number three and a half is coming soon which is nice. It just eats a lot. By a lot, I mean it likes to have a slice of cake for pre-breakfast because you can't eat on an empty stomach. And it expects breakfast pudding. If it wasn't so tall I'd think it was a hobbit. But, in its favour, it knows how to work the DVD player which is much more than us.

Going to leave you with a picture of a watermelon which I have nurtured with my own fair hands and some flowers and stuff because I can be soft and fluffy once in a blue moon. Be good kids, lots of love ♥

## Day: I need a drink.

We ran out of stuff to watch on Netflix and Prime - well anything we could actually agree on anyway. So, after much 'discussion' we are now watching the Sweeny series from 1974! Talk about going back in time! The wallpaper, the hair styles, smoking in an office and the pubs, using a phone box, flares! It's fantastic! We also watched the new Sweeny film and the old one too. Rod is now wandering about the house saying 'you're nicked' and 'give us a fag guv' in his best saarrfff London accent.

We finally finished the jigsaw! All 3000 bloody pieces of it and, staggeringly, it was all there and not a piece missing! It's taken nearly four months and the dining table has been out of use so it's just as well the weather is marvellous and we eat outside. I'm going to frame it and stick it on the wall because a) we are never going to suffer that level of frustration again and b) I would quite like the dining table back.

Rather grossly, Rod found what looked like number two's on his bedside table in a blob on his watch. On closer examination it would appear it's bat poo! I know we have a 20ft high ceiling in the bedroom and there is plenty of room in the roof amongst the insulation but having bats pooing on us in the night is really not my favourite thing. Saw a film once where the bats turned into vampires at midnight and did dreadful things to the guests in an hotel - don't suppose they would come anywhere near me as they probably recognise one of their own but I don't fancy Rod's chances much.

Cats are now pushing their luck. Nigella likes to sleep on the sofa in our bedroom so I put a rug there to keep the sofa clean so the little sod has taken to sleeping on the armchair. Peter the black kitten has become quite bold and sits there looking at me until I feed him. It's quite creepy - being stared at by a black cat. He's definitely witchy and I can feel him watching me. His ginger brother, Menelaus, is much more timid. Rod says we should have called them Harry and Meghan...

Diet is going well - lost a stone and a half. Still look like a cross between Bubbles De Vere and the Loch Ness Monster from behind but it's a start. I did have a glass of wine last night - first in about three months - but I won't be causing a surge in Smirnoff shares anytime soon. As my body is obvs now a temple, (albeit akin to the Taj Mahal) and as my teetotalness has contributed massively to the reduction in my derrière, I'll reluctantly stick to water.

Apart from that, this week I've made a birthday cake, knitted baby stuff, written a play, had my nails done red, emptied out our 'don't throw that away - I might need it' drawer, planted petunias, made broccoli and Stilton soup and talked to a little kid without it crying.

Love to you all, have a splendid weekend and just be kind

# Day: I think it might be the purple lizards after all.

It's all been a bit full on over the last week or so which accounts for the lazy day I'm having today. Let me quantify just how much of a melt I'm being...fed the cats. Made a double decker fish-finger and boiled egg sandwich, squeezed three oranges (that was hard work - turning the juicer on) and am now where I have been all day, blobbing out in bed, watching Netflix. With crumbs stuck to my bottom obvs.

Had a couple of things to do back in England so Rodders decided we would drive back and leave at 7am on Saturday morning. He's usually really cruel and sets the loudest alarm possible and turns every light on then pulls the covers off me whilst I lay there groaning. But, I was up at 6am (two sixes in a day! Who knew?) showered, dressed, packed, ready and even made coffee to go in our millennial friendly refillable cups! He was staggered! We actually left eight minutes late in the end and he only held it against me for about three hours.

Reached our favourite hotel in the Basque Country called something beginning with G. It's the most incredible place - full of antiques and locals talking in xyz's and g and j's. And lions. They have a thing for lions. Not real ones obvs just huge statues everywhere. Rod does look a bit knackered in the picture below but to be fair he had just driven from Portugal to Spain then the Pyrenees.

Up with the lark(ish) then off through the border and on

to France. Finally arrived back in Folkestone, in bed with sandwiches from the garage (they were M&S darhlings obvs). Another early start to see the Dentist who cheerfully explained how he was going to extract a cracked tooth, then cut into my jaw and chop off a lump of sticky out bone. He promised that the stitches and bruising would all be so painful afterwards I wouldn't be able to eat. Finally, there is a God! I'm going to be skinny!!

Anyway, there was that, I'll go back in a few weeks and have it done - so excited! Instantly booked a flight home because, let's face it, Algarve - Folkestone??? No contest.

Did my maternal duty and had dinner with Brat No. 4 which was nice but quite enough of all that. It was fairy useful though and did, without much moaning, do my favourite rummage through all the charity shops in my never ending quest for priceless treasures. I bought a tea set for our new kitchen because everyone needs a multicoloured teapot.

Met up with friends and had ginormous pizzas (I ate every single bit). Very pleased to be home on Wednesday night via Luton Airport. I always want to say 'were you wafted here from paradise?' when anyone mentions Luton Airport but unless you are old like me you won't know what I'm waffling about.

First job was to feed the bloody cats who magically appeared as I unlocked the front door. Nigella was definitely pissed off at having to sleep on her cushion in the concrete mixer instead of the sofa in our bedroom but she'll get over it. Had a chat with the moggies then watered the garden and obvs had a chat with the butternut squash and the aubergines. I was doing that talking to myself menopausal woman thing again as I wandered around the supermarket but it's OK because no one knows when you wear a mask.

I have a confession - I was weak and led astray by some terrible ladies who forced me to drink vinho verde. And, I pulled ! Admittedly, he could have done with a bath, was three sheets to the wind and about six stone overweight and was a total pain in the arse. He was eventually escorted from the premises but I think Nikki would have flattened him if he'd stuck around. I didn't know that all my friends are alcoholic, cackling witches but my face hurt with all the laughing. I think it was possibly the conversation about designer vaginas that finished me off.

Rod's being a Nancy and has tooth ache and had to see the doctor but hopefully will be home soon. FaceTime is OK but not the same as a cuddle. On the plus side, I can have fish finger sandwiches for dinner and watch what I want on Netflix.

I promise to be all motivated and may even get up before *Homes Under the Hammer* tomorrow. Maybe.

Peace and love to you all ♥

Peter and Menelus

## Day: Red or pink nails this week?

Feeling very sorry for myself this week. Woke up last Sunday and Frankenstein was looking back at me in the mirror. This whole tooth and jaw thing has gone bananas again. Not only did I have a golf ball sized blob of gunge under my chin but another one had appeared on the side of my face. Actually, it was more the Elephant Man with mumps. Soho, off I toodled to see the chaps at Loule hospital.

First thing they do is zap your forehead for temperature with this ray gun thing (think *Star Trek*) which beeps and buzzes if you aren't normal. Well, obvs I wasn't normal (shock horror) and the nice lady pressed a panic button (I shit you not) and a swat team materialised. They escorted me into a room (not a padded cell) and eventually ascertained that my temperature was due to the face full of pus rather than covid 19. Anyway, poked, prodded, needles and prescriptions later, I've spent the last week in bed, (high risk sepsis) moaning and groaning and closely inspecting lumps to monitor shrinkage.

I've been so lethargic and knackered with the knockout pills so all I've done all week is knit and watch the telly. Today is the first day I've been able to open my mouth properly so it's been a week of dribbling and disgusting table manners. Menu has been a bit limited but I've rediscovered the delights of microwave fish fingers and mashed egg sandwiches. Not together obvs.

Nigella is not impressed with my laziness. She comes

meowing up the stairs, sits there moaning at me until I feed her and then disappears until she's hungry again. She has discovered she likes playing with my wool when I'm trying to knit. She's just like the Brats when they were little - only ever want to talk to you when they want feeding or when you need the loo. I can't even do that in peace any more - go to the loo without Nigella rubbing against my legs (which is a trifle inconvenient) or she sits and stares at me until I've finished - rude. I don't even like cats.

Had the remote to myself this week whilst Rodders has been away. On the one hand I have missed his delightful company but haven't missed his snoring or poppy bottoms. I never do either of those things obvs. I softly tinkle and sprinkle unicorn glitter. It's been lovely chatting to friends for hours on end. Men don't understand that women can talk about everything from the best way to roast potatoes to the exact location of their G Spot and if it was a bullseye last night or not in the same conversation.

Shakespeare said, 'I am wealthy in my friends.' I am truly blessed with you mad lot. Much love ♥

*Day: I need a cuddle.*

As I searched for change to buy a car parking ticket on Tuesday, I wondered why my brain is so disorganised. I mean why am I not one of those women who have a trolley token on their key ring? Why do I have 789 million bags for life in the car but not one of the buggers when I'm in the queue at Lidl? Why don't I look in the cupboards before I go shopping? Why don't I write shopping lists? Why do I buy loo rolls every time I go shopping and now have enough to see to the bottoms of the entire population of Portugal for the next six months? Maybe I'll start with a trolley token and see what happens.

The tooth thingy continued this week until Wednesday morning at 10am when a very nice dentist injected my jaw lots of times and I woke up an hour later dribbling and unable to speak. (No change there then from your average Saturday night/Sunday morning.) Dr Joal gave me a little box containing the tooth and a lump of bone but sadly the tooth fairy is away in England so I'll have to save it! Can't say it was my favourite thing this week but, miraculously, my delicate and petite gob is no longer full of pus and gungy stuff. Apparently, don't laugh, I am classed as vulnerable and need close attention - maybe doc meant in a nutcase/psycho kind of way? Anyway, thankfully it's all over and healing well which means a huge reduction in medication so maybe the occasional shandy might be on the cards?

Brat No. 3 turned up on Tuesday. It kept ringing for a lift from the airport so I had to bite the bullet and collect it. Must admit, it has been fairly useful already - it brings me coffee in the morning and can do stuff on phones and computers. Apparently it's not the Bee Gees that make your phone work, it's GB's and you have to remember to turn them off when at home or they run out. Who knew? Made it a cake and as long as it's fed on a regular basis, it seems quite tame.

Went for a walk on the beach last night - such a beautiful sunset. Had a paddle, water was really warm but didn't go in for a dip as didn't have a cossie with me. And, let's face it, no one needs a tsunami to ruin their evening. Wondered why the bed was full of sand this morning. It gets everywhere - perhaps the key is not to be a scabby cow and have a shower before bed?

All the excitement of the week has caught up with me so going to have a nap now. Oh how my Fridays have changed!

Have a shamazeballs weekend kids. Be kind, thoughtful, apologise, and spread a bit of love because it's all you need and makes all the difference. Life is far too short to be unhappy.

# Day: What if this is actually a 13 year old alien boy's science experiment and we are in a jar on a shelf in his bedroom?

Does anyone have a recipe using butternut squash? Currently have approx 3 million of the little blighters expanding daily in the garden. Possibly because I forgot I'd planted some seedlings then planted more thinking they were courgettes. If anyone would like one pop by and help yourself. Afternoons only obvs as I won't be alive in the morning and certainly won't have showered, be dressed or presentable in any way and, let's face it, no one needs that kind of negativity in their life.

Actually did some housework this week. I dusted stuff. Well, it was past the point of dusting and had to be washed because it's been about six months since the last time. To be fair, we do have loads of priceless treasures (shit) including two wooden parrots, three sombreros and four Zulu spears adorning the walls of the kitchen which do generally look better without the thick layer of dust usually covering them.

Been vaguely productive this week. Managed another chapter of the book I'm currently attempting to write. A friend asked me what it was called and was horrified but I think 'The Fall and Rise of the Sunshine Cliteratti Society' is quite catchy. Picked the last of the figs and bottled them in red wine, cinnamon and ginger. Pickled eggs and beetroot, tidied our bedroom up (three weeks of slatternly behaviour in Rod's absence) and even did the ironing. Wrote several articles and book reviews, made a carrot cake and was on time twice this week out of about ten appointments which is incredible for me.

Brat no.3 says that as it's now 28 years old I really don't have to say 'be a good boy' to it when I go out. I'm only attempting to be maternal but would appear only succeeding at being irritating. Moi? It has also realised that when I say 'please pass the thingy' it could be a tea towel or the cat. It says menopausal, middle-aged mothers are special, very special...see below.

Peter the kitten has decided he likes me. Or maybe he's just a mercenary little bugger who has worked out it's me who does the feeding. He ate some ham from my hand under the watchful supervision of his mum and now comes into the kitchen and watches me. I talk, he listens and never answers back which makes a change for a man, mentioning no names...

Anyway, starting preparations today for Rodney's Return after three weeks of absence. Takes longer than it used to. One or two (3000) grey hairs to attend to, mustachios to pluck (never using Veet on my face again - I had a red beard the pirate and tash mark for a week) other bits of hair removal by various methods (TMI) but it's a bit late for liposuction and a tummy tuck as he'll be back Monday. Made him a carrot cake and put his special red knickers on the top of his pile of budgie smugglers.

Anyhoooo, thought I'd spoil you with a couple of pics of me posing in my new dress which is a size 16! Bought some classy black leggings in Primani in an 'L' rather than the 'XXL' of last year. No bleach stains on them yet but there's still time.

Have a shamazeballs weekend and be good to each other. Kindness is free kids. Love.

# Day: Wonder if this is the beginning of a Zombie apocalypse?

I've discovered a telly channel full of ancient wonderful stuff. Currently watching Lovejoy - should finish the lot by the time Rod returns from another quick trip to the UK. All he took was a clean pair of knickers, an electric toothbrush and a 5 litre wine box. Happy days.

Brat No. 3 could possibly be my current favourite child. I sent it a WhatsApp message asking nicely for a coffee and it did! I'm still working on the 'be a good boy' and 'take a jumper with you just in case' comments because it is 28 but I read somewhere that mothers are supposed to demonstrate maternal stuff. Not sure what that's all about - maybe I need to read volume two? No.3 is a very happy bunny as it's better half has arrived here in sunny Portugal. It's a Kiwi and absolutely fabulous. No.3 is definitely punching.

Jalapeños have gone bananas this week. Well, obvs they aren't bananas - they are curly peppers but you know what I mean. Loads of them so we now have jars of jalapeños preserved in oil and vinegar. Also made some chilli sauce which is a bit blow your bottom off but very tasty. I do like all this growing and gardening stuff. It's peaceful ignoring the world whilst listening to an audiobook and digging holes or pulling out weeds. Especially if you put headphones in and people assume you can't hear them so don't talk to you. Marvellous.

Had an issue with white hair (I'm old) which had to be dealt with. Unfortunately the only colour they had in Lidl was aubergine so well it's a bit, purple ish - think Mrs Slocombe. Rod laughed and said I had a purple head, little sweetie. So I'm posting this picture of Rod in a sombrero for revenge.

Woke up to find Nigella staring at me. Then she started meowing and saying 'mum, ffs, feed me you lazy cow' so I did. All I got in return was a look of disdain before she pooed in the petunias.

I've decided to turn over a new leaf and become organised. Starting with shopping. I've got a trolley token in my purse and am writing a list as I run out of things. It won't last but I promise to try. Currently have oranges and cake stuff. I know what I mean. If it's successful going to try the being on time thing but let's not get ahead of ourselves.

Had a lovely night out with some fabulous ladies who all have alcoholic tendencies. A beautiful warm evening, sitting outside under an orange tree. It's a bit wonderful living here and I do count my blessings.

A little bit of sadness I'm afraid. A couple of weeks ago a lovely lady we know who lives here in the Algarve suffered a fatal brain haemorrhage. She was only 53. The system here is that you opt out of organ donation so people were helped as a result because this wonderful lady did not opt out. May her memory be a blessing 🖤

A little thought and kindness can be the difference between life and death.

## Day: Here we go again...

Having Brat No. 3 here has its bonuses. Not only does it make coffee on demand but, it can do magical stuff with computers and the little people who live in my phone and iPad. In fact, after being shown how to about 9647,777 times, I can now do a hyperlink. Is that right? Does one 'do' or is it 'insert' or 'make'? I come over all glazed eyes and befuddled (normal really) whenever technology is mentioned if it's more complex than changing from Prime to Netflix.

Woke up in the night last night (bladder - 53 - you know the struggle girls) and the bloody cat was sitting on Rod's pillow looking at me. Shock nearly brought on a tsunami of the pee variety but I managed to shuffle to the loo just in time. Then Nigella decided to have a chat, at 3.30am. Doing that whole miaow thing and rubbing her tail on my feet (no duvet - hot flush) she was not going to stop until I hoisted myself out of bed, into the kitchen and fed the little monster. Then she just buggered off - not a backwards look. Rude. Don't even like cats.

I've been watching Lovejoy on TV - so dated! First series was filmed in 1986 - the year the first brat appeared. No internet, no mobiles, CD's had just arrived and definitely no social media. Up to 1993 now and that big hair! It's fabulous - all perms and shoulder pads! Found this pic from 1983 with Brat No. 3. I suppose it was quite nice.

As you may have gathered, I do have an aversion to kids.

Well, most of them apart from a select few of the little monsters. There is one little ratbag I do actually dislike less than others and it's his birthday so obvs I was a good auntie and made him some cakes to take into school. There are so many e-numbers in these red and blue cupcakes the kids will have to be scraped off the ceiling. I don't care - just going to sit back and watch and laugh.

It's been another beautiful day here and a lovely start to the weekend seeing these loons whilst doing cake delivery. Nigella is pleased to see me upon my return home, as usual. Enough excitement - time to water the garden accompanied by a glass of orange juice and an audiobook. I do fancy half a bottle of vodka with my orange juice but as my body is now a (quite large) temple I shall refrain.

Have a splendid weekend, lots of love and happiness to you all 🖤

Brat no. 2

# Day: Butternut Squash Soup, Roast Butternut Squash, Butternut Squash Pie...

Anyone been watching *Roadkill* on iPlayer? The Prime Minister in the series is called Dawn. Just putting it out there. It would be a laugh and let's face it - I couldn't be any worse.

Ate my own body weight in sushi on Monday whilst having lunch with two of my favourite girlies. What with the steak last night at Rui's with two other of my lovelies, (and Rod who is dashing rather than lovely) my bottom now resembles the Himalayas rather than the rolling hills of the Cotswolds. But, hey ho, more of me to be fabulous at fifty (ish)!!

Not really sure how it happened but Nigella seems to have become just a little too comfortable. Not only has she decided she likes Rod's side of the bed, but, she ate my breakfast. Well, I say breakfast because it's the first meal of the day and just because it's at about 1pm that doesn't make me a bad person. And, breakfast (and dinner) in bed is relaxing after a stressful morning watching Lovejoy. Actually, since Rod's return (that sounds like a Catherine Cookson novel) last week, I haven't managed any Lovejoy so am at season five and a bit. They're now using mobile phones and not phone boxes and his mullet has been chopped off so we've finally arrived in about 1994!

In other exciting news, I made chilli and tomato jam which

is pretty shamazeballs. Brat no. 3 eats all the stuff I produce and hasn't even objected to the butternut squash saturation situation. Saying that No. 3 and 3.5 are apparently not dining with us tonight - possibly because it spotted me holding yet more of these terribly versatile vegetables and is taking the easy way out.

Had the gang round for dinner on Sunday and one, who shall remain nameless, offered to clean my oven for me because it's so disgusting. I'm not proud and absolutely no offence was taken. Actually, I am trying, (very trying) to be organised and now have two trolley tokens. Obvs I left them in the car with 763,980,763 bags for life but little steps and at least I have them. Being a domestic goddess is overrated. I'll stick to the 'that'll do' school of housewifery, as the brats and Rodders will testify.

Took Brat 3.5 to the Chinese shop to peruse the vast array of treasure on offer. Whilst I enthused about the leopard print and diamanté, it chose not to purchase anything of that ilk - absolutely no taste.

As I'm sure you all know, October is National Breast Cancer Awareness month. You may recall, (possibly because I moan regularly about my various ailments) that I was a right drama queen and went through this a couple of years ago. Anyhooo, was very pleased to hear from a friend who also went through all that malarkey that she's had the five year all-clear which is marvellous news. I'm not there yet but, as you know, only the good die young so I expect to survive another few centuries. So, would you all do something for me please? Have a fondle, poke, prod, wobble and generally check out those boobies and balls and dangly bits and do it to each other too. Obvs explain to your chap/missus first or it could be a tad awkward. The chart below tells you how to check and, just to scare the hell out of you I'm posting a dreadful photo of moi and the reality of cancer. Love and kisses.

Baldilocks

*Day: Never, ever, ever, drinking again.*

Having broken the news to Rodders that, upon publication of my Lockdown Diaries into a real live book, he is about to be catapulted into international super-stardom, his reaction was fairly predictable. He never listens to me anyway - well, you wouldn't if you were him would you? And, as he was busy scanning iPlayer for the *Antiques Roadshow* at the time, his response was slightly less enthusiastic than I would have liked but priorities prevail and I quite understand that auntie Enid's chipped vase takes precedence or perhaps it's Fiona Bruce? Hmmm...

I'm waiting for the call from Hollywood to buy the film rights. Wonder who they'll cast as me? I see myself as a Julia Roberts type but have a feeling Mama Cass would be more appropriate. Anyhooo, I'm terribly excited and thank you all for your wonderful kindness.

Apart from being in the running to win the Nobel Prize for Literature, have mainly been the most embarrassing mother ever imaginable, hot flushes have gone through the roof (just as well because Rod always moans able the heating bill) and we have a new addition to the family. You know about the first thing - I'll try not to mention it more than six times a day - and, those bloody hot flushes are horrendous. Actually, I think they might be a kind of gentle hint from Lucifer to remind me of things to come if I don't pull my socks up. Well, in my case I probably need to put in a tad more effort than just new sock elastic but let's not go there for now. We are the proud parents of another beautiful fish to add to our collection. This one is called Frango, which means chicken. Stay with me... Frango used to live with a lovely man called Dennis and Dennis has a really weird surname we can't say but Frango is vaguely near enough. As we already have a frog called Dennis, we decided that having a fish of the same name would be far too confusing so Frango the Fish is soon to be resplendent upon the kitchen wall. He's not a real fish, not even a dead one, (OMG! I am far too irresponsible to look after living things! Ask the brats). Actually, he's probably really a fruit bowl but who's counting?

May have possibly had one too many at the weekend - Ok, I was bladdered, plastered, sloshed, inebriated and it's fair to say, fell under the wheels of the wagon. Luckily, my menopausal/drunk/middle aged memory is so rubbish that my faint recollection of being in a cocktail bar and seeing various friends and brats, 3, 3.5 and their chums, is all rather hazy. I do, however, recall telling 3.5 that I was going to be her matron of honour and wittering on about a hat before being dragged away by Rodders who I'm sure regrets buying me that last margarita.

In other news, I fear we may have been usurped as Nigella's favourites. Actually, cats are even more fickle than men so I shan't pay too much attention and am not ever the slightest tiny bit bitter that Nigella prefers 3.5 to me.

I know life is a bit higgledy-piggledy at the moment so if you feel a bit rubbish and fancy a chat or if there is anything I can help with, please ping me a message and I'll do my best to cheer you up. I can only remember one joke but you will love it! Lots of hugs and big love xxx

PS: It's a bit chilly here in the evenings now - Rod's had to resort to socks with his sandals!

Brat no.2 and 2.5

Day: where's the nearest AA meeting?
Asking for a friend....

This menopause thing is playing havoc with various bits of me. Mainly things like where the hell did I put my purse/phone/keys/wine? and the sweaty bits. I know ladies are supposed to glow but a) lady is questionable and b) not like a nuclear reactor. Poor Rod - I haven't managed to have dinner for about three years now without stripping off. It can be embarrassing but I think he's getting used to me being mainly naked 90% of the day, and night. I think he'd just rather it wasn't when having dinner with friends in a posh restaurant and knocking my wine over in the process.

And, I shoplifted. Not on purpose because if I was going to it would definitely be for more than a three euro mascara from Lidl. Popped it in my bag for life thing that I had actually remembered for the first time this year and there it was amongst the fish fingers (my favourite food in the world ever) and non-alcoholic wine (in your dreams) when I was unpacking. You could have knocked me down with a feather - honest.

So, apart from that I smell rubbish all the time. I must do with all the 'glowing' I do. Rod hasn't actually said so but we are both a bit rank and lazy when it comes to it but, there are nights when you just can't be bothered and we have a little sniff of each other and think sod it. Gross.

In other startling news, we found a priceless treasure tucked away at Kit and Caboodle which is definitely my favourite shop in the whole of the Algarve. It's seriously the best thing in the world because it's covered in parrots. I love this shop - full of one-off pieces of stuff you just fall in love with. Let's face it kids, everyone needs a parrot covered towel box thing. And a pink rug. And, a chandelier for the kitchen. If it was a leopard print chandelier with diamanté it would be perfect but I'll just have to make do in the meantime.

Brat no. 6 managed to injure itself whilst walking the dog. What a div. Actually, it fell over a log and ended up needing stitches. No. 6 told No. 4 it was a wild boar or a massive bear or maybe a Yeti and the even more divvy No. 4 believed it. Seriously.

The butternut squash thing is finally over but seems to have been taken over by aubergines. I'm going to make a Moussaka every night next week and probably the following week too. Can you make wine from aubergines?

We seem to have a lovely indoor water feature every time it rains. Rod has been up on the roof in an attempt to dam the Panama Canal flowing down the bedroom walls. It's a bloody long way up but he survived the ordeal and fingers crossed the next torrential downpour won't necessitate the need for an umbrella as we sleep.

Nigella has become even more of a diva. She has no boundaries and I can't help feeling that we've been shit parents and spoiled her. Cats have this way of saying 'f**k off' with a look which is a cross between the devil and Margaret Thatcher about to announce a cabinet re-shuffle. I've told her not to sit on the car, or the white bedspread, or the dining chairs, or the kitchen work top. She ignores me and I have to bleach stuff - it seems to work for her.

I may have mentioned that I'm about to become an even more fabulously famous internationally fantastic author. Did I even mention it? Anyhoooo, the book cover (or jacket as we lovies 😂😂😂 call it) is in the planning stages. I'm thinking maybe Marie Antoinette meets Cruella De Vile in an allotment might be a starting point but I definitely need some butternut squash and a 5 litre wine box as a reflection of my personality. Fair?

I just remembered something else ridiculous and I'm positive it was purely a menopausal slip rather than a one way trip to the loony bin (can I say that these days?) Anyhooooooo, am I the only one who talks to everything including the dishwasher? I loaded it, put the cleaning thingy in, it wooshed and farted then I found a spoon in the sink and popped it in the dishwasher. I actually heard myself say 'oops, sorry, forgot something' as I shut the dishwasher door. Let's just think about that for a minute - I apologised to the dishwasher for disturbing it. Yeah....

Bloody caterpillars 🐛 have attacked my Brussels sprouts. Little buggers literally stripped every bit of leaf and green bit. I shouted at the little sods but that didn't really help so washed them off with vinegar and fairy liquid. They haven't actually eaten the sprouts themselves, even bloody caterpillars don't like Brussels. Then I fell over. Spectacularly. Pulling weeds out that were rather stubborn so I was pulling really hard, really really hard then the clump of weeds gave way and I fell backwards, legs in the air and rolled over the edge of the wall and landed in a bag of compost. Which was nice. Bruise on my thigh developing into a purple and red blob and, even more serious, a broken nail. Very dangerous stuff gardening. Anyone need aubergines, let me know. Unless of course you can make wine from them in which case they are all mine. Obvs.

I'm doing a yoga class next week. If I survive I'll let you know how it goes. It's a morning class which is totally unnatural and possibly even illegal. Maybe I should take a hip flask just in case?

Have a splendidly happy day and remember, it's so easy to be nice. Love you all, big kisses 💜💋💋

Brat no.1

# Day: Could I please have some vodka with my ice?

Today kids we are going to talk about my ailments. This hot flush thing is driving me bonkers because one minute I'm laying in bed with Rodders, holding hands under the covers, 😣😣 all snuggled up and watching something age appropriate (the *Antiques Roadshow*) and suddenly, whoosh! A bloody tsunami attacks me from the toes up and I'm shoving the duvet on the floor, reaching for the max switch on the fan, leaving puddles on the parquet, (sweat, not pee - I'm not that old) and waving my vast nakedness around in an attempt to cool down. Then, after five minutes when the bedroom has finally reached a temperature suitable for polar bears to move in, I'm cold and am wrapped up in a 15 tog duvet. I had a little moan about it this morning when rudely awoken by yet another hot bloody flush (I say morning but I think *Homes Under the Hammer* had just finished so cutting the A.M. thing a bit fine...) anyhoooo, Rod (bastard) said, 'You're like an old banger with a knackered radiator' so it won't be hard for you to guess whose toothbrush I will be cleaning the loo with tomorrow.

You may recall (but you probably won't because I'm sure this unmemorable drivel just fades from your consciousness as you scroll down to something much more interesting - The Life and Times of The Lesser Spotted Maggot or similar), that I became a lady last December. Obvs, those who know me well will strongly deny and object to this fact but, bear with.

I clearly don't mean in the sense that I have stopped behaving like a fishwife when inebriated or I'm safe to put on speaker phone (don't do it) but that I am now an actual real-life lady. I am a descendant of King Robert the Bruce after all! In fact, it's just a bit of fun to help support a beautiful castle in Scotland which is such a fabulous and worthwhile cause.

Because I have delusions of grandeur of the highest degree, I informed the bank of my change of title and they have now reissued the appropriate bank card which I shall take great delight in using at every opportunity. I had to send them a copy of the Deed of Entitlement (I shit you not!) and the chap at the other end of the customer services helpline even called me Lady Annandale at which I just giggled but tried not to let him hear - like I was really used to it and being bowed and scraped to was something I just accept as normal - obvs we didn't talk about my overdraft because that would just be unseemly.

Nigella is unhappy and has made her feelings quite clear. She likes to sleep upstairs, on the sofa or our bed. During the summer that was OK because she could get in and out through the windows. Now of course, it's chilly at night and shut windows mean she's had to make alternative arrangements. I have never seen such annoyance on the face of any animal as she manages! Cat-flap needs to be fitted pronto or I can see a mutiny on the horizon. Our neighbours have a new kitten that someone dumped in the bin so they have brought it home and it's now tiny but healthy. It's very bright ginger and called Speedy Gonzales. Personally, I would have called it Ed Sheeran Gonzalez or Ron Weasley Gonzales but each to their own.

I must go - Ladies Night Out to prep for which is going to be tough going in the time available. Why is the hair on my head coming through white and the mustachy and mole stuff black? Taking Brat no.3.5 with me to meet the coven so I'll be on my very best behaviour-ish.

Have a groovy one, love always

Brat no. 3 and 3.5

# Day: My Smirnoff shares seem to be doing well.

We did that old people thing at the weekend - went for a drive. My grandparents used to do this complete with Thermos flask, folding chairs and the Express for Grandma, Times for Grandpa. We modernised the same thing - glass of wine (glasses) and phone. Had a stroll along the beach at Quarteira; right along to the end (not up the slope because I can't quite manage that bit) and back again. Beautiful day, fabulous view, one of those happy to be alive days. Or maybe it was just the vino??

Momentous event - the orange tree produced two oranges which I lovingly squeezed then savoured every sip. We planted the tree two years ago so fingers crossed there might even be enough for a jar of marmalade next year! Rod planted a lemon tree (gin/vodka requirement) which is now more of a twig but we live in hope. Very excited about the avocados which are coming along nicely. I might open a market stall at this rate.

Peter and Menelaus have finally stopped running away from us every time we appear (I can understand that) and now ignore the cat food but come in and beg for ham. (Clearly not Jewish cats). They like those rank tinned sausages too and will now eat little bits from my hand. They still eat their proper dinners but only once we've gone to bed and there's nothing else. Speedy González from next door has joined their gang and it's quite sweet watching them play until they poo in the petunias and

I shout at the little sods.

Plans are afoot for the cover of my new book - these musings of tripe and drivel I pretentiously call The Lockdown Diaries. Had a makeup trial which was hilarious because obvs it has to be exaggerated and dramatic. I look like Ursula from *The Little Mermaid*! The complete look is fab - I can't wait to share the end result with you. It's a sort of combination of Bet Lynch/The Wicked Witch of the West/Cinderella with cats and butternut squash.

I lost a chicken the other day. Cats were watching me as I was prepping dinner. Put a chicken in a Pyrex dish then needed the loo. Me, not the chicken. I could see the little buggers licking their lips and as I cook like a Tasmanian Devil has wooshed through the kitchen and there was nowhere to put the chicken, I shoved it in the empty dishwasher. Did the loo thing, washed my hands whilst singing happy birthday and continued devastating the kitchen. Could I find the bloody chicken? Noooooo. I mean how can you lose a chicken? Had a glass of wine, tidied up, had another glass of wine, took the washing in, had a glass of wine. Dirty dishes seem to have arrived in the sink so upon opening the dishwasher there it was, one chicken. I even said 'Bloody hell, where have you been?' to it. Rod said, pardon? But I told him I was talking to the chicken and he just said, oh. I think he ignores me these days and just says things like, yes darling, at regular intervals in an attempt to convince me he is actually participating. Totally understandable.

So kids, have a marvellous day and don't do anything I wouldn't. No boundaries there then. Mucho love 🖤🖤🖤🖤🖤

# Day: Is there a wine box price comparison website? Asking for a friend.

Surpassed myself with the whole maternal thing this week. Finally remembered that Brat No. 6 had had a birthday so pinged it new bank card details on the family WhatsApp thingy. Actually, thinking about it, that'll do for all of them so maybe extra Mama gold star for being early or do I have to remember all of them? When they were younger I did blag being a good mother but now they are all too old for me to get away with it. I used to be able to go to a school thing and as long as they saw me and I waved whilst they were doing the nativity or carol concert or murdering London Bridge is Falling Down on the recorder, I could leave with a vaguely clear conscience. I did make cakes and do the PTA but was always one of the mothers drinking wine rather than tea at Sports Day. I know - how surprised are you?

The other maternal thing I managed this week was the purchase of advent calendars and delivery prior to December 1st. I actually surprised myself but a) they were on special offer by the till at Lidl and b) Amazon is a marvellous thing. It's a start. I keep telling them kids are just not my thing but they insist they are my offspring so what can I do?

No.3 and 3.5 are finally leaving us after a few months here in the Algarve. Obvs it's totally understandable because would you want to live with me? Noooooooooo. So, they are off to sunny Lisbon next week for their next big adventure. I may even miss them a tiny bit but obvs not much. 3.5 can cook, load the dishwasher and put the washing out so it's a keeper.

Weather has been proper Book of Revelations stuff this week. Wouldn't be at all surprised to see Noah floating around but my cabbages and marigolds seem to like the biblical flooding. Rod has discovered that the Niagara Falls deluge down the kitchen wall is actually from roof tiles that have a huge gap and are generally wonky so he's been up on the roof being cross and fixing things. He has been very busy this week - being a lumberjack and chopping up logs with the assistance of no. 3 and a chainsaw. Wood was from an old dead olive tree but wasn't quite dry so the wood burner struggled. However, nothing that Rodders and his flame thrower couldn't resolve. I shit you not. there I was, making dinner, chopping or stirring or something housewifely, and there was this blazing inferno coming from the corner of the kitchen! Chaps love playing with fire - I think it's the caveman in them.

In other startling news we had a trip to the Chinese shop. I love these shops - you can literally buy anything. We bought some radish seeds, a rug for the bathroom and some diamond earrings. I'm rubbish with earrings - always lose them so the 1 euro 50 version Rod treated me to this week are really quite lovely. We need another rug to match the parrot blanket box in the upstairs bathroom but Rod made a vomiting face when I picked up the bright pink one so I'll wait until he's next away.

Next door had a bit of a disaster and their wall was washed away in the torrential rain. A friendly little dog turned up in our garden having escaped through the collapsed wall so we brought him inside because his mum was out. He had really tiddly short legs so we called him Napoleon. After Napoleon had eaten Nigella's dinner and was snuffling about for more food, I gave him some ham and he settled down in front of the fire until his mum collected him. I may be one degree closer to Rod agreeing to us having a doggie....

No.6 six always likes to call its' Mama and share special moments. This week I was treated with a video of a daddy sheep having a lovely time with a mummy sheep whilst No.6 was taking its dog for a walk. Makes me feel so special and simultaneously realise that men never progress past about twelve years old.

My ten year old computer is knackered (bit like me) so a new laptop, keyboard and mouse have been purchased. Rod and I just looked at it all and then along came 3.5 and did stuff so it now works. I can't type on a laptop because I'm old and the laptop is English and the keyboard Portuguese so how confused am I? Do you know how long it's taken me to find a comma and a question mark?

Anyhoooo, tonight 3.5 is cooking so I don't have to do anything other than push the button on the wine box. Have a marvellous weekend and look after each other. Much love kids.

# Day: Are we doing 2021 or not going to bother?

I can't stand shopping. In shops, with people, trying stuff on, being all sweaty and hot then cold, screaming kids, lugging bags around...purgatory. So, I don't usually bother unless it's life or death. Against my better judgment, I went to the local shopping centre which is huge. Bumped into a friend (Miss K) so had a good reason to stop shopping and go for a drink instead. Now, Miss K is a German lady, is single and is rampant. She's the only person I know to have been banned from Tinder. I shit you not. We had a chat about her recent dating experiences which involved lengthy details incorporating the use of various German sausages. You get my drift? It all seems like so much hard work.

Took Rodders to the airport and off he went to the UK looking miserable. He was fine by the time he'd reached Folkestone thanks to several large G&Ts and a bottle of red. I didn't get out of the car at the airport and snog him, much to his great relief, as was wearing my slippers and dressing gown. It was a bit touch and go leaving the airport because you have to put your ticket in the machine to raise the barrier. Thank you Lord for automatic barriers!

Before his departure, Rod made a cheesecake. He went shopping for ingredients on his own and it was fabulous. I washed up but you can't have it all.

Brats 3 and 3.5 have abandoned me too. Gone to Lisbon to

have an adventure which is marvellous. It's rather quiet here with just the cats. But, I do have the remote for a week.

The roses are looking beautiful - in a rare moment of slush Rod bought me seven rose bushes for our seventh anniversary. He ignored our eight. He won't forget the ninth... They are such a deep red and loads of them. The planters are full of cabbages and cauliflowers so I can see us living on piccalilli and vegetable soup for several months in the not too distant future. NASA would have fun trying to explain the sudden appearance of a methane cloud over the Algarve.

Looking forward to our book group Christmas do tonight. And, I have a chauffeur so I might just have a second glass of vino... or six.

Found these pics of Father Christmas with brats 4 and 5. It's only 10 days to Christmas Eve so I suppose I'll have to vaguely think about stuff soon. Or just tell them all to order something from Amazon or is that not really entering into the spirit?

I know it's all a bit rubbish right now so be patient and kind. Lots of love 💚

Brat no. 1

# Day: Crimbo Extravaganza

Happy happy Christmas kids! Bit of a weird one for many and I do appreciate being able to spend the day with brats and friends. And Lawrence the dog. He seemed to have a lovely day or it could just be the Turkey he took a bit of a shine to. Santa was a bit late and hungover; didn't drop the stockings off until about 8 this morning and was wearing a dressing gown very similar to mine but that's just a technicality.

Rod bought me an elephant for Christmas. We've called him Noel and thought he would probably be happier living in Africa with his mum and dad than in Portugal with us so we'll have to pop over and see him when we can. Besides, the only bed that's big enough for him is ours and that could be a bit awkward. Rodders also bought me some perfume so I am surmising he thinks I smell and is trying to get me to move to Africa to be with Noel. Understandable.

Apart from that, Brat no. 3 decided that it would be a sensible idea to have a swim in the sea at Quarteria. I drank wine and watched. Strange brat. No. 3.5 is used to Kiwi Christmas days and BBQs but was quite taken with our turkey and all the bits. And, it's a bit of an alcoholic like me so we get along famously!

Rodders was particularly chuffed with Santa's crimbo effort - tickets for the Rugby League Challenge Cup final - think I might have earned a few brownie points for that!

We entered in the spirit of things and actually had a Santa

loo seat cover. Not been peed on yet but there's still time.

No.4's mutt joined in the festivities - a smiling chihuahua in a Santa outfit is always a bonus. It's even smiling and posing for the camera.

We played charades and one of our guests (who was pissed and couldn't be arsed) did *Jaws* every time. Shocking lack of effort and we need a sober re-match. I always do *Bridge over the River Kwai* just because my Grandpa always did.

No. 6 took the doggies for a walk, and they celebrated in Germany with 6.5's family. No.4 was with 4.5 (might as well adopt 4.5) in Kent in their bubble and it was a jolly day for everyone despite the current nuttiness.

I'm going in search of left overs now - really fancy some turkey and stuffing!

I feel truly blessed to be able to have spent a wonderful day with family and friends and realise that many of you aren't so lucky. From our home to yours we wish you lots of love and let's all hope that next year life is back to normal, unless the aliens get here first!

Mucho love ♥

## Day: Enough of this Drivel!

And so , my darlings, the time has come for me to knock these inane ramblings on the head. 'Thank f**k' for that!' I hear from all around the world! Since I've become all international superstar, well, I will do when this old bo**okcs is published and Hollywood starts casting. I will obvs be far too busy and important to spend time on this garbage.

We've decided to make some New Year Resolutions and see if we can last more than a week. I did consider getting up before *Homes Under the Hammer*. Took three seconds to dismiss that idea. I'm going for a walk each day, either on the treadmill (on speed one - let's not get too excited) or just a ten minute wander around the grounds. (One should regularly survey one's estate - the staff need checking up on or they forget their place - especially the foreign johnnies.) Rod is going to stop doing poppy bottoms in supermarkets and blaming it on me. We thought we'd leave world peace and clean up the oceans until next year.

Well, what a pickle 2020 was! Obvs 'pickle' is an euphemism for total f**ktard, cataclysmic, zombie apocalypse stuff. I'm not going over all that fighting for loo rolls, washing your hands whilst singing happy birthday and how much my Amazon and Smirnoff shares have rocketed in value. There were many wonderful things that happened during the year too - it wasn't all doom and gloom. I love the pictures on Facebook of families finding the time to walk by the canal or along the beach.

Wildlife has come back with a vengeance, rivers and streams are cleaner and people are actually checking on their neighbours. I adore the photos of the arts and crafts kids have been learning - used to love a bit of finger painting or cupcake decorating with six brats whose speciality was making necklaces from pasta. No 6 had a thing for crucifying it's Action Man. I don't think it still does that stuff.

We had the most wonderful wedding and several babies put in appearances. An engagement, an extension, lots of lovely visitors, six cats, butternut squash, petunias and aubergines.

From us to you, we wish you love and happiness, and hope. How can you not have hope when you look at the future all wrapped up in this beautiful photo of my new baby cousin, Nova. Thank you all for your friendship and kindness - you all mean the world. 💚💚💚💚💚👏👏👏👏👏👏👏

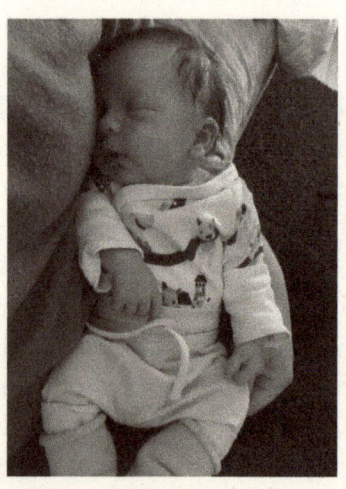

Baby Nova

# Acknowledgements

Blimey, where do I start? I only began writing this diary because I was bored and it filled the time between getting out of bed and having my first drink of the day. Now look at me, being all publishy and discussing sales figures and book jackets.

You lot have kept me going through all this stuff, I really mean it. Some days when I feel all rubbish and knackered and can't be arsed I drag myself over to the computer and tell you about planting courgettes and them turning out to be chili peppers and life seems all worthwhile again.

I need to say some thank yous or I will never be spoken to again. The Brats and their .5's have been jolly good sports - bloody hell - you would need to be as a child of mine. Rod gave up reading this tripe ages ago and just disappears into his shed and mends something instead or builds another extension so he can say he's far too busy looking for a monkey wrench or a tin of tartan paint.

My lovely girlies far and wide, Gingers Lunchtime Gang, Jill in NZ, Jan in Oz, Lou and Karyn, Stef-Fanny for being helpful with everything inappropriate, all my beautiful nephews and nieces and now great nephews and nieces. (Cheers for that - still don't like cats or kids.) Susi and Martin, big kisses. My lovely ladies here in the Algarve - you sustain me with wine (Lesley), funny stories (Maggie), Anne - you are definitely the sensible one and Andrea who listens to me blathering on about rubbish on a regular basis. My Book Club Ladies, (and Roy) and, Helaine, your constant support and kindness is rather marvellous. Writing Group (apart from Jon who is just a div).

I feel a bit like I'm doing an Oscars speech and want to thank my therapist and my nail technician but I don't actually have the first one and the second one is actually quite crucial in the scheme of things. The team at The Conrad Press; eternal gratitude, especially James and Charlotte. Talk about patience! Olga, your cover photos are shamazeballs and you are a shiny star. Much love.

There is one very special lady I want to say a huge thank you and give a massive hug to, Ann Brittain. Ann encouraged and persuaded me to do something with my ramblings and despite my reservations and her constant loveliness, I did and so you have her to blame! Thank you Ann, I probably would have thrown the towel in a long time ago without you.

You lot have been kind and wonderful - I am truly blessed in my friends.